BODYLINE CASUALTY

The Bert Oldfield Story

BODYLINE CASUALTY

The Bert Oldfield Story

GAVIN GLEESON

Foreword by Rick McCosker OAM

Published in 2025 by Ginninderra Press,
Melbourne, Australia
www.ginninderrapress.com.au

Copyright © Gavin Gleeson

A moral right of the author has been asserted

All rights reserved. This book is copyright. Apart from any fair dealing for the purpose of private study, research, criticism or review, as permitted under the Copyright Act, no part of this book may be reproduced by any process without written permission. Inquiries should be addressed to the publisher.

Typesetting and cover design by Workingtype Books

ISBN: 9781761099243 (paperback)
ISBN: 9781761099250 (ebook)

ACKNOWLEDGEMENTS

In the making of this book I would like to thank the following:

Karin, Gretchen and Konrad Sussmann for their generous recollections of their grandfather which have been invaluable.

Debbie Lee and Mandy Wolbers at Ginninderra Press for their amazing support and giving a first-time writer a chance.

To Col Fletcher for proofreading and Rick McCosker for giving his time so generously in writing the foreword.

Peter Nelson, Roy Rose, Gurvinder Singh Gill and Talisha Godwin for their encouragement and belief.

My wife Katrina for everything (including proofreading), my children Mikayla, Georgia and Benjamin and my parents Harold and Lynette – particularly Mum who used her powers of coercion to motivate me to get the manuscript off a hard drive and out into the open.

For Katrina

CONTENTS

Acknowledgements v
Foreword.. xi

Adelaide Oval, 1933.. 1
Making the Grade 5
For God, King and Country 13
Polygon Wood 21
The A.I.F. Cricket Team 29
The Baggy Green 39
Undertaker's Understudy 47
The Roaring 20s 57
Then Came Bradman.. 71
An Enduring Partnership 87
A Great Depression 93
Calm Before The Storm 105
Fast Leg Theories 113
Bodyline..123

The Battle of Adelaide 137
Was Oldfield Facing Bodyline? 151
The Wounded Warrior 155
The King of Keepers 167
Bowling Maidens 181
The Accidental Captain 187
Saviour of Lions 195
Peter Pan of Cricketers 201
The Final Session? 213
Holiday in Nazi Germany 225
Back in the Slouch Hat.. 229
To the Close of Play 239
The Final Account 249

W.A. Oldfield Playing Record... 255
Bibliography 257

FOREWORD

Bert Oldfield certainly had a story, one that has lingered on and is still of much interest today – he was an integral part of one of the most talked about and written about periods in the history of cricket.

This game called cricket has brought together so many people from all walks of life, ages and backgrounds and is the reason I have been asked to pen this Foreword. It has given me much pleasure to do so.

I met Bert, or Mr Oldfield as I respectfully addressed him, at his Pitt Street Sports Store not long after its establishment in the early 1970's. Having moved to Sydney from my home in Inverell, I was now playing for New South Wales. I needed to purchase more gear and it was recommended I go and see Mr Oldfield. I remember him as a very dapper little man, friendly and interested in hearing of the start of my First-Class career. Many of my peers who were playing for New South Wales at that time had similar experiences of meeting up and chatting with him.

Given my abiding love for the tradition and history of cricket, I read this story with a great deal of interest. I quickly found that there was much common ground between myself and the subject of this biography. We had both faced challenges when playing on matting wickets. Bert initially played for Glebe in the Sydney Grade competition, which was the forerunner to the old Sydney Club that I played for, and we played on the same ground, Jubilee Oval at Glebe. We both debuted for Australia in an Ashes Test on the Sydney Cricket Ground.

And of course, we both subsequently incurred head injuries in significant Test matches, after incorrectly attempting a hook shot. In my case, the ball fell onto the stumps, and I was out, both literally and figuratively. After having spent two days in hospital I was able to return to the dressing room and was then able to bat in our second innings -something which would not be allowed today under the concussion rules. There was none of the political turmoil of Bodyline that had been associated with Bert's injury, as mine was just a case of incorrect technique and not the fault of the English fast bowler, Bob Willis.

Unfortunately, history and the media often focus on those events when there is more to be told. Gavin Gleeson has certainly achieved this with a well-researched story informing the reader that there was much more to Bert than most people were aware of, including myself.

Mahatma Gandhi once said, 'Strength does not come from physical capacity; it comes from an indomitable will', and this is evident in this story. Gavin has well captured the human fears that Bert would have lived with through his war service, and when representing his state and country particularly during that tumultuous era.

This is a wonderful walk-through of Australian history, of how England countered the mastery of Bradman, of the Baggy Green, of friendships, triumphs and tragedies, and includes a courageous effort by the author to describe the wedding day and the bride's attire!

I commend this thoroughly researched and enjoyable book to all readers, not just cricket fans. Knowing so much more about Bert Oldfield, I now feel that our meeting all those years ago has taken on far greater significance – thank you Gavin.

Rick McCosker OAM

ADELAIDE OVAL, 1933

He tried to shake-off thoughts of home. Walking into the relieving shade of the portico, through the archway into the refuge of sandstone and russet brick, sounds of the girls playing, but here he stood drenched in sweat in intense mid-afternoon summer sunlight with nowhere to hide. Time to focus.

Wringing the salty damp from his piercing grey eyes, he glanced at the scoreboard high on the hill with pupils like pinpoints – 'WICKETS 7...Oldfield 41...TOTAL 218'. Twirling the bat in his hands, he calculated that the team was 123 runs in deficit, with hope starting to fade. Well into the tail now with Tim at the other end, it was up to him to at least draw level.

In all his years, the game had never been like this. Indeed it was part of the sporting theatre for touring teams to play the role of the pantomime villain – this was different. The Adelaide establishment shaded under ochre-coloured grandstands and the general public crammed standing-room only at the mercy of the relentless sun, questioned the parentage of members of the England Cricket Team in unison until their throats were grazed. Ravaged by deprivations from years of economic depression, another thing that they loved that provided escapism and enjoyment – was being taken away. The narrow oval felt like it was bulging inwards from a tide of flushed faces and mad-eyes – ready to pounce if the Englishmen put a foot wrong.

The unmistakable figure of England captain Douglas Jardine: unsmiling, all nose and chin – paced around like a police inspector staring intermittently at Larwood who was equally silent. There was no confusion in their unspoken dialogue, Jardine's irritation was Larwood's admonition to hew harder at the horizontal coalface of compacted clay and distressed couch grass. Larwood was shark-like, an unsettling blend of terror and beauty. His physique and action were compact, efficient and engineered to precision.

Close enough to tap him on the shoulder was the ever-present Gubby Allen at short-leg. He surveyed the field of men concentrated behind his back and the apologetic smile from Gubby confirmed it would be another head-hunter. He had been employing a vertical bat to the bouncers to shield his chest and face but the risk of a ricochet to one of the catchers was too great – against all the wisdom of the game – to play each ball on its merits – he resolved to hook the next one.

Framed by the Adelaide city skyline, Larwood set into motion. Momentum building step-upon-step like a soundless avalanche until his left foot pounded the crease like a striking hammer. In the blur of his right-arm – the ball dematerialised. Scanning frantically Oldfield tried to locate it as he swung the bat aimlessly. His vision filled with a distorted smudge of flecked gold and red leather as the projectile crashed into his skull.

Deafening darkness and searing pain; he had been here before... at another time, in another conflict. The bat was cast away into irrelevance, as he clutched at his Baggy Green cap to scoop-up what he felt was his fragmenting head. Falling to the ground, he clenched his eyelids tightly as if to stem liquefied brain matter.

Fading in and out, he heard disembodied voices barely audible above the intensifying fury of the crowd. "I'm sorry Bertie", a Nottingham *accent reverberated in the darkness. He remembered Christ's teaching: blessed are the peacemakers. "It's not your fault, Harold". Opening his eyes, there was an assortment of shuffling white leather boots...he closed them again.*

The agonising sensation dulled faintly as his right temple now swelled and pulsated. He felt a hot trickle down his right cheek...was it sweat? Was it blood? Helping hands propped him into a sitting position and his wound was bathed with a soothing trickle of water and lightly dabbed with a towel. Immediate concerns for his own survival shifted to the emerging reality of the deteriorating situation swirling around him. Hostility and the looming threat of violence hung on his actions. He could no longer salvage a mere innings, it was beyond that now, it was up to him to save so much more.

"I'm alright, help me up". Aided onto shaky feet, he drew upon what few reserves he had left to remain standing – his head throbbed violently. The intensity of the crowd's anger was briefly calmed as audible gasps of relief swept around the ground. Like an apparition, the form of Australian captain Bill Woodfull came sharply into focus out of the afternoon sun. Dressed in his dark suit, the teacher by profession looked like he was striding firmly onto the school yard to admonish a group of quarrelling boys. Instead upon arrival, his captain summoned him gently, "come now, Bertie".

The pair walked off the ground to swelling applause as he wiped blood and sweat from his flushed face. His spiked boots clattered all the way up the stairs as he passed an apprehensive Bill O'Reilly exiting the dressing-room – his turn to fill the breach.

As the volcanic roar re-erupted outside, he collapsed to the floor.

MAKING THE GRADE

John and Mary Oldfield welcomed their newborn son, William Albert Stanley into the world on Sunday 9 September 1894 in the Sydney suburb of Alexandria. Now in their early-40s, this seventh child would be their last. Favouring his second given name, little 'Bert' was the baby brother of Richard, Maude, Beatrice, Lyle, Linda and Jack.

John Oldfield was born in 1853 in Manchester, Lancashire and specialised in the upholstery trade. After emigrating to Australia, he worked for furniture retailer Farmer and Company in Pitt Street, Sydney. Mary Ann Oldfield (nee Gregory) was from the southern tablelands region of NSW and was born a year earlier than her husband.

The family of nine lived in a rented four-bedroom Federation-style cottage named 'Cotswold' at 17 Allen Street, Glebe Point, a working-class area in Sydney's inner-west. Still standing, the property has a chequer pattern tiled path leading through a tiny yard on to the red brick cottage which has a prominent bay window in the front room overlooking the garden. By 1910, John Oldfield had decided to go into business on his own using 'Cotswold' as his base and started to advertise his

'Cotswold' 17 Allen Street, Glebe Point.

upholstery services regularly in the trades section of the *Sydney Morning Herald*.

Young Bert attended Newtown Public School, a four-kilometre trek from the family home, passing Sydney University along the way. In customary short pants, he would carry a tennis ball to keep himself amused on the lengthy commute – bouncing it on the pavement and rebounding it off walls. After transferring to the Cleveland Street Superior Public School in Surry Hills, he developed a love of cricket but had to settle for yearningly looking-on at the school yard matches played by senior students which he was frustratingly excluded from. Only upon moving to the Newtown Superior Public School, which had a formalised cricket program overseen by a sports master, that he was able to start playing organised cricket.

During his teens, Oldfield became attracted to the role of wicket-keeping and wore the gloves for the St. Stephen's Newtown church team in the Western Suburbs Junior Cricket Association competition. "I do remember clearly that keeping fascinated me from the start" wrote Oldfield in his 1953 biography *The Rattle of the Stumps*, "I was certainly bitten by the bug early". He likens the attraction of a certain personality to the wicket-keeper role as having the similar 'crazy streak' of a soccer goalie and describes "the thrill of uttering that almost barbaric shout of 'howzat?!'". Ironically, Oldfield's 'Keen Fielding' medal from his St Stephen's days would remain the only fielding-specific trophy he would ever win.

Outstanding wicket-keeping performances in the sport of cricket are invariably overlooked, unless it involves a spectacular diving catch or masterful stumping that draws everyone's notice and admiration. High-quality neat and efficient keeping often goes unacknowledged mostly due to inattention, however the dropped catch, the fumbled run-out attempt or the error resulting in 4 byes will draw the wrong kind of scrutiny to a gloveman. Thus Oldfield was not deemed a child prodigy unlike his future teammates Donald Bradman, Alan Kippax, Archie Jackson and Stan McCabe and largely flew under the radar throughout his teens. His shortness in stature and slight frame favoured wicket-keeping as did his characteristic tidiness and attention to detail. Oldfield stood up to the stumps in the days before grilled helmets on suburban concrete wickets covered with green coir matting where the ball could rise or shoot violently off the matting surface, canvas trim and leather strapping. Upon reflection, the veteran keeper said of those formative junior cricket experiences, "no doubt I missed a lot of chances, but there is equally no doubt that by the hard way I learnt a lot".

Shortly after achieving his school leaving certificate, 17-year-old Oldfield commenced working life, appointed as a clerk to the traffic branch of Sydney's tramway system in September 1911. He continued playing in the NSW Churches Cricket Union competition into his late-teens with the Newtown Methodist side until at the age of 19 he decided to try his hand at playing for higher honours. Joining the local Glebe District Cricket Club for the 1913-14 season he would make his entry into the Sydney City and Suburban competition – a level below the three tiers of Sydney Grade Cricket. Playing against an eclectic group of teams such as the Union Bank, Gordon Veterans and the YMCA, Oldfield donned the maroon and blue of Glebe in his fourth-grade debut on Sydney's Domain.

Having spent two decades as the seminal hub of cricket in the new colony which saw military and civilian clubs clash in a primitive form of the Australian game, Hyde Park in central Sydney relinquished its position to the more spacious nearby Domain in 1856. A year later the Domain hosted Sydney's first intercolonial cricket match between New South Wales and Victoria and in 1862 a contest between the home state and an English team. By the eve of the First World War the ground had at least two pitches in

The Sydney Domain

operation for lower grade games. Playing as a batsman, Oldfield made an impressive 84 runs on debut, the joy of which gave him great hopes of working his way up into the first grade team which included the likes of Test players Albert 'Tibby' Cotter, Charles Kelleway and Warren Bardsley.

Early in the 1913-14 season, Oldfield rotated between fourth and third grade teams making an initial impression with his batting. In November, he knocked 65 in Glebe's 8 for 220 in a draw against Double Bay. Promoted to third grade in December 1913, Oldfield scored 55 unbeaten runs in Glebe's nine wicket thrashing of Paddington at Wentworth Park but failed with the bat the next week against Redfern with a paltry 7. Back with the fourths in the week before Christmas he made 68 not out in Glebe's 217 against the YMCA.

A belated Yuletide present, which became the first of many slices of luck in the rise of Bert Oldfield, awaited him upon his return to the third-grade team on 27 December. In the absence of the regular keeper Harold Frazer, he seized his opportunity and volunteered to step into the breach. With the stumping of a Redfern batsman to his name, Oldfield recalled that he, "[had] performed in such a manner that the captain asked me to keep the position". The New Year yielded mixed results batting-wise with a duck against St George, 49 against Petersham and top scoring with 28 in a low-scoring match against University in the final round in April, but in the end Oldfield consolidated his position as keeper of the thirds.

As the weather cooled in Sydney and cricket gear started to accumulate dust in the bottom of musty cupboards and garden sheds, news of conflict in the Balkans began taking up column inches in the newspapers after the assassination of Austria's Archduke Franz Ferdinand in Sarajevo by a Bosnian Serb nationalist on 28 June 1914. After a month of diplomatic turmoil Austria declared war on Serbia sparking an escalating crisis engulfing most of the northern hemisphere. Australia pledged its support for Britain, but down in the harbour city on the other side of the world, it all seemed very far away.

The winter of 1914 was equally tumultuous for the Glebe District Cricket Club thanks to the departures of key players and lean recruitment options available. In a preview of the club's season prospects in the *Sydney Morning Herald* of 30 September 1914, the loss of three major players was lamented but Oldfield was identified as one of the key junior players, "expected to take a share in restoring the balance".

Oldfield found himself promoted to the seconds as the talent-depleted club launched the 1914-15 season campaign, but his fortune in elevation did not translate to riches with the bat. In October, he was dismissed for 10 against Redfern at Jubilee Oval in Glebe and in November scored only 4 at Birchgrove Oval against Balmain – but did effect a stumping. By mid-December, the Hurstville-based St George club was once again his nemesis as he was dismissed for 1 and 0 and did not trouble the scorers with zero keeping dismissals across two weekends. By the end of 1914, over 52,500 Australian men had volunteered for the conflict in Europe but it had not greatly affected the numbers in Sydney Grade Cricket.

Oldfield's luck had turned following New Year's 1915 with an undefeated 34 batting in the middle order and adding to his stumping tally against the Leichhardt navy blues on Leichhardt Oval. He was starting to capture the eye of the first grade selectors

Wentworth Park, Glebe

by February, with tidy keeping and batting – scoring 34 and 69 not out against North Sydney at Wentworth Park.

After almost two full seasons, Bert Oldfield's dream came to fruition on Saturday, 20 March 1915 with his selection for the Glebe club's first XI. With an extraordinary array of past, present and future Australian cricketing talent, it would not be a run-of-the-mill grade match – it had a feeling of a grand final. Former Australian cricket captain Syd Gregory (of the famous Australian cricketing dynasty which included his Test Captain uncle Dave Gregory), was captaining Waverley a month short of his 45th birthday. Gregory had debuted in Test cricket way back in 1890. Adding to the strength of a formidable Waverley side was NSW and Australian wicket-keeper Hanson 'Sammy' Carter, state off-spinner Walter Pite and future batting stylist Alan Kippax.

Another of Oldfield's opponents that day was the wide-eyed, round-faced 19-year-old Norman Callaway from the country town of Hay in the far south-west of N.S.W. The previous month Callaway had exploded onto the cricket world by blasting 207 runs in 214 minutes with 26 boundaries on debut against Queensland at the

Sydney Cricket Ground. Glebe's captain and 20-Test veteran Warren 'Curly' Bardsley found the Wentworth Park pitch to his liking and chose to bat after winning the coin toss. Bardsley blazed 146 opening the batting with Glebe reaching 305; Oldfield only making a very modest contribution of 6 runs batting at nine. Glebe took the upper-hand with both Waverley openers dismissed for ducks prior to stumps, getting knocked-over by fast-bowler William Cullen who made his only NSW appearance alongside Callaway. Waverley resumed its shaky innings the following Saturday with its captain at the crease hoping for consolidation.

Resuming his innings on zero, Gregory only added 3 runs before Oldfield caught him off a strangled ball down the leg-side off future NSW fast-medium bowler Ted Forssberg- a dismissal that would become a cherished early highlight for the diminutive keeper. Glebe eventually won the match on first-innings points despite Norman Callaway's top-score of 90 in Waverley's 185. His brush with Test wicket-keeper Hanson Carter in the Waverley match made a big impression on the rookie who resolved to emulate the veteran's neat and snappy keeping style.

Now in the upper echelon of the Glebe club, Oldfield attended the 6am training sessions on Jubilee Oval under the coaching of Warren Bardsley's father, William who had also been influential in the development of Glebe's Test players Kelleway and Cotter. Committing to the athletic lifestyle, Oldfield prioritised his physique – eschewing smoking and drinking –taking long walks and conducting deep-breathing exercises to increase his lung capacity. The final round of Sydney Grade Cricket for the 1914-15 season in mid-April enjoyed what the *Sydney Morning Herald* described as 'ideal weather' which favoured the bowlers. Glebe just passed Sydney University's 116 at University Oval with 2 wickets in hand with Oldfield (7 not out) at the crease for the winning runs.

FOR GOD, KING AND COUNTRY

A FEW SHORT WEEKS into cricket's yearly hibernation, reports had been flooding back of Australian troops storming the beaches of the Gallipoli peninsula on the Dardanelles Strait in Turkey back on 25 April. The stories of valour, a feeling of duty and sense of adventure motivated many Australian men to join-up for the war effort. By the Glebe District Cricket Club's annual general meeting in July 1915, six members of the club had enlisted in the Australian Imperial Force including Harold Frazer, who Oldfield had replaced back in third grade, and the club's Test players Albert Cotter and Charlie Kelleway. Oldfield was elected to the club committee, the first grade selection committee and as the first grade secretary, but he would not fulfil these duties for very long.

Two days before turning 21, the minimum age required for enlistment in military service without parental permission, Oldfield left his job with the tramways and enlisted at Victoria Barracks on Tuesday, 7 September 1915. The examining medical officer recorded the slightly-framed recruit's particulars: fair hair and complexion, grey eyes, 5 feet 5 inches tall (165 centimetres) and weighing 138 pounds (62.5 kilograms) with no physical or

Private Bert Oldfield

mental obstacles for service. Oldfield confirmed his religious denomination as Church of England and his mother Mary as his next-of-kin.

The following week, he reported for basic training at the Liverpool military camp on the outskirts of Sydney. The Liverpool camp had been the subject of recent controversy in which the conditions of the neighbouring internment camp housing Germans were considered more favourable. There had been a long-time military presence in Liverpool with a barracks for British troops located there since the early 19th century. Prior to the First World War, visiting Field Marshal Lord Kitchener recommended a permanent camp and training facility be based in the area, but after a handful of years in operation it became the subject of a Royal Commission in 1915.

The Commission headed by Justice George Rich was launched in July and heard that the camp had a scarcity of uniforms and overcoats for the winter as well as a shortage of rifles and ammunition. Rifles that were on-hand were often faulty when on the rare occasion there was shooting practice. Recruit accommodation, which had initially been tents, were replaced by 'draughty' huts, mattresses were in short supply and food was being stored in accommodation areas. The hospital standards at the camp were also condemned and the sanitary conditions were simply described as 'bad'. It was noted that in comparison: "[the] men in the German concentration camp... had comfortable bunks, and were well supplied with overcoats". By the winter, conditions in the camp had become pitiful with recruits succumbing to colds through inadequate clothing and shelter. When recruits eventually received medical treatment they would often have to bring their own bottles for the medicine to be dispensed in. Food-wise, there was little more than tinned corned 'bully' beef to eat, with breakfasts often having to be scrounged. It was an appalling situation for men who had walked away from their civilian lives and careers in the name of duty to be confronted with. The fact that men like Oldfield still enlisted despite the well-publicised shortcomings of the training camp makes their decision even more admirable.

Among Justice Rich's recommendations handed down in late-August, were that a permanent administrative and medical staff should be established at the camp including an armoury and better processing of new recruits. Wide-ranging improvements were suggested for huts, kitchens, bathing houses and latrines, including the installation of electric lights. It was further recommended that all public houses within a 5 mile radius of Liverpool should be prevented from selling liquor to soldiers after 6pm.

Liquor restrictions would not have bothered the teetotaller

Oldfield, but he may have been spared its previous deprivations with reforms being hastily implemented during his time there. In late October, the press reported "quite a metamorphosis". An account by a local resident of Parkes who visited his brother in the camp detailed in *Western Champion* of 28 October declared that the Liverpool camp was now "laid out like a town, with streets", but that they may have overdone the tree-planting, "[t]he camp is wonderfully improved though. There are regular kitchens there, nice and clean...[e]verything is much better, and there is little room for grumbling now".

Basic training at Liverpool included instruction in the use and maintenance of the Short Magazine Lee Enfield Rifle, bayonet practice, infantry tactics, methods of unarmed attack and defence, marching drills and physical training including running and callisthenics. Two –thirds into his three months of basic training, the command determined that recruit Oldfield would be appointed to the Australian Army Medical Corps. Upon attestation back at Victoria Barracks on Tuesday 14 December 1915, Private Oldfield was assigned to the 1st Australian Dermatological Hospital based in Cairo and embarked for Egypt on the *Kanowna* six days later. A keen photographer, Oldfield sent snaps back home to his family in Glebe Point from ports-of-call along the voyage. Spending the first of many Christmases away from home on the troop ship, he arrived at Suez and travelled onto Cairo which was full of newly-evacuated veterans of the Gallipoli campaign.

The 1st Australian Dermatological Hospital was based in a sprawling fort built by Napoleon Bonaparte following his invasion of Egypt in 1798 in the inner-Cairo district of Abbassia. For a regular church-goer and a young man who had still been living at home with his parents prior to enlisting for service it could be imagined that Oldfield found his duties somewhat confronting.

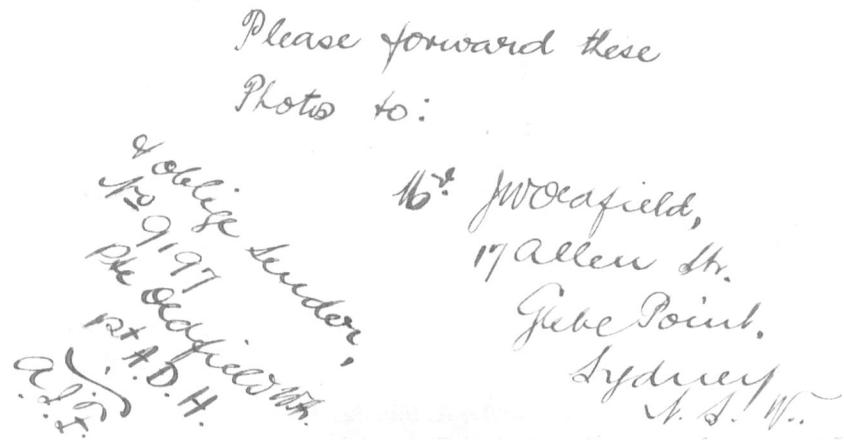

A letter Bert Oldfield sent to his family from abroad.

The overwhelming function of the dermatological hospital was the treatment of venereal diseases contracted by Australian servicemen in the brothels of Cairo.

Bored and homesick troops awaiting embarkation for the next conflict zone set-up cricket matches often in rough desert conditions with a pitch of coir matting rolled over bare earth and dry, barren outfields. An Ashes-style contest saw British regiments play an embryonic Australian Imperial Force team boasting the likes of Tibby Cotter (who would be killed in the Battle of Beersheba in 1917), Dr Eric Barbour, A.G. 'Johnnie' Moyes and Ted Long. The Australian Army Medical Corps in Egypt had its own cricket competition played between clubs from the different hospitals including the 3rd Auxiliary Hospital, Heliopolis, 4th Auxiliary Hospital and staff teams. The hub of the Saturday competition was Cairo's Gezira Sporting Club which had its own picturesque cricket ground, now the Club's number 1 soccer field. Once an exclusive outpost for the British Empire's sporting pursuits, the sprawling green oasis also included polo grounds, tennis courts and a golf course.

⁂

Very little has been recorded of the incident which occurred on 14 August 1916 which found Oldfield locked-up in the bowels of the old fortress. In what appears to have been an out-of-character incident, he was charged with neglect of duty, namely – insolence to a non-commissioned officer and on 16 August was sentenced to eight days incarceration in the Abbassia detention barracks. It may have been a comfort for a disillusioned Oldfield cooling his heels in the dungeon of the old fort to know that his time in Egypt was coming to an end with the 1st Dermatological Hospital's relocation to England soon underway.

From late September 1916, Oldfield continued his duties in the new location of the Parkhouse Camp outside Salisbury, a cathedral city in the county of Wiltshire, until earning a break from treating syphilis and gonorrhoea with a detachment to the nearby military hospital in Bulford from October 1916 to May 1917. During his time at Bulford, Oldfield's increased training and medical exposure was building for eventual service as a stretcher-bearer. By operating under the Red Cross flag wearing the Red Cross (or SB = Stretcher Bearer) armband, Oldfield joined a tradition of battlefield medical service covered under the Geneva Convention of 1864 where as a non-combatant he was offered a degree of protection. If an enemy deliberately targeted him while wearing medical insignia, it would be considered a war crime. Bert would not be the only child in the family who answered the call to join the war effort with elder sister Linda May enlisting as a staff nurse in the Australian Army Nursing Service on 22 May 1917 at the age of 29. While initially sent to Egypt, she served in the general hospital in Salonika, Greece until the end of the war, returning to Australia in 1919.

On 1 June 1917, Oldfield sailed to France via Southampton and was assigned a week later to the 15th Field Ambulance where it was on non-combat operations near Albert in northern France. He became one of the reinforcements for the unit which had suffered 13 casualties during the 2nd Battle of Bullecourt. Also falling at Bullecourt on 3 May 1917 was his Waverley opponent Norm Callaway who died at the age of 21, his First-Class average forever an extraordinary 207 – a young life full of potential tragically extinguished.

The 15th Field Ambulance relocated to Contay, west of Albert, to establish a corps mumps station before moving once again to the village of Sercus in northern France in early August 1917 as further preparations were made for an impending offensive involving the 15th Australian Infantry Brigade.

Apart from the occasional chance to play a scratch match of cricket behind the lines, Oldfield's life in France was tightly regimented with half-hour physical training following Reveille at 6:30am, breakfast at 7am with parade and kit inspections following during the mid-morning. As the unit's deployment approached, examination of medical equipment intensified: each stretcher-bearer was directed to carry 48 hours of rations, a blanket and a waterproof sheet.

POLYGON WOOD

The Battle of Passchendaele, also known as the Third Battle of Ypres, was an attempt to capture the strategically-important high grounds on the south and eastern sides of the Belgian city after 3 years of attritional stalemate in the region since the early days of the war.

The offensive was launched across the Flanders front on 31 July 1917 and by 20 September the 1st and 2nd Australian Divisions had begun their advance along the Menin Road sector, making history along the way as it was the first time two Australian divisions had participated alongside each other in a campaign. It was also the first time Australian forces had spearheaded an offensive. Weeks of advancing and weathering blistering German counterattacks edged the Australians to the south-west fringe of an area known as Polygon Wood.

An irregular quadrilateral-shaped pine forest, Polygon Wood was surrounded by rolling Belgian paddocks about 8 kilometres east of Ypres. Roughly the shape of an ancient arrow-head that pointed north-east, at the tip was a small plateau known as 'The Butte' upon which the German forces established a headquarters and observation post reinforced by bunkers and concrete pillboxes with machine-gun crews.

The job of advancing across the remnants of Polygon Wood and capturing the German vantage point in a 'bite-and-hold' strategy was assigned to the 14th and 15th Brigades of the 5th Australian Division. While under the direct command of the 5th Division HQ, Oldfield's 15th Field Ambulance was nominally supporting the 15th Brigade which was under the charge of legendary Brigadier-General Harold 'Pompey' Elliott. Following the calamitous Battle of Fromelles in July 1916, Elliott wept openly at the destruction of his beloved 15th with casualties amounting to 1776 men. The 5th Division lost 5513 men which at the time was the worst loss of

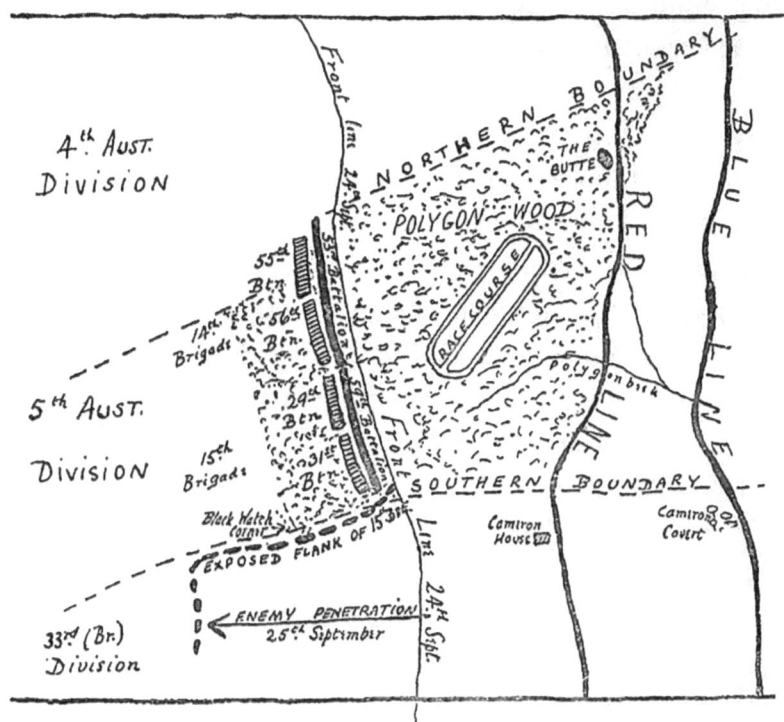

Polygon Wood battle map.

Australian troops in a single operation until it was surpassed by the Battle of Bullecourt.

After 3 years of war, barrage and counter-barrage, the pleasant pine forest of Polygon Wood was now an apocalyptic landscape of utter oblivion. The once-tall pines were reduced to denuded stumps, twigless and fractured. The chocolate-brown soil which once lay beneath a blanket of pine needles was now pockmarked with shell-holes and piles of splintered debris.

On 25 September 1917, Bert Oldfield was at Clapham Junction, a hotly-contested position during the Menin Road battle just under a kilometre south-west of Polygon Wood – now a staging post for the battle to come. In much the same way as the transport hub in south-west London, Clapham Junction was buzzing with activity and had a single hastily-built rail-line to bring supplies to the front. Reminiscent of the work of wartime photographer Frank Hurley, Oldfield took his own dramatic photograph of Clapham Junction with columns of helmeted troops filing past a British Mark 1 tank covered in camouflage netting. Multiple shells exploding on the horizon of the photograph corresponds with war historian C.E.W. Bean's observation that the Germans had been shelling the front of Polygon Wood "viciously" since 23 September.

Despite the benefit of surging momentum for the British, preparations for the offensive did not go entirely smoothly. On the night before the attack, the Germans launched their own operation on the lines of the British 33rd Division made up of the 98th and 100th Brigades to the right flank of Oldfield and his 15th Australians. The attack was eventually repelled but serious doubts were held about the ability of the 98th to go on the offensive the following day. A tense situation was becoming even more concerning when very few reports came back from the blindsided British to clarify the situation as zero hour approached on the morning of 26 September.

In the pre-dawn, the 15th Brigade took their positions outlined by tape-laying parties in no-man's-land. Fortune favoured them as the tree stumps of Polygon Wood obscured their movements despite the frequent volley of German flares. The 59th Battalion spearheading with the 29th and 31st closely behind, lay quietly in the southern half of the wood with Oldfield and his comrades of the 15th Field Ambulance behind them awaiting the commencement of the creeping barrage at zero hour.

At 5.50am the artillery descended, the creeping barrage was described by CEW Bean as, 'the most perfect that ever protected Australian troops'.

"It seemed to break out, as almost every report emphasises, with a single crash. The ground was dry, and the shell-bursts raised a wall of dust and smoke which appeared almost to be solid. So dense was the cloud its near edge, could not be distinguished. Roaring deafening, it rolled ahead of the troops "like a Gippsland bushfire." Its very density carried one disadvantage; in such a fog, it was difficult to discern where the actual line of shell-bursts lay, except by running into them. Direction has to be kept by officers with compass in hand".

As the 15th Brigade rose and carefully crept forward behind their explosive curtain the four-man stretcher squad readied itself at the rear. They were Private Bert Oldfield, the 23-year-old tramways clerk and club cricketer from Glebe Point, Private John Callon an ironmoulder from Stoke-on-Trent, Staffordshire who enlisted in Brisbane, the baby of the group Private Arthur Joyce, a 19-year-old budding pathologist from Sydney's Rose Bay – they were led by Lance Corporal Roy Quirk from the seaside suburb of

Manly. Carrying bandages, field dressings and a folded wooden stretcher, they scanned the battlefield ahead for injured and tried to hear above the cacophony for calls of assistance.

With vision obscured by the churning wall of dust slowly approaching them, the German defenders atop The Butte randomly fired their machine guns and rifles into the bursting cloud hoping the rounds would hit the unseen enemy. Oldfield and the 15th Brigade had an added problem. The 98th British Brigade on the right flank, depleted from the night before was struggling to keep up with the advance leaving the flank exposed to a German stronghold called the Jerk House from which machine gun and sniper fire was being directed over what these days is a potato paddock onto Polygon Wood.

The area became a deadly killing ground for all who found themselves there with direct frontal machine gun and rifle fire from The Butte and enfilade fire from the right flank. The creeping barrage from the British could be just as deadly as the precision of the countering German artillery if an eager attacking line mistimed their advance.

In an attempt to bolster the floundering right flank, the 57th Australian battalion was brought up from reserve, but according to Charles Bean, "had met the full German [counter] barrage, which fell behind the attacking troops". An infantryman, Private James Daly of the 57th Battalion who had reportedly been hit by an artillery shell while sheltering in a crater with others, was placed on the stretcher of Lance Corporal Quirk's stretcher team. The squad turned and rushed him away from danger headed for the regimental aid post located near the Hooge Tunnel, a two-mile underground system which offered safety and medical treatment. What would happen next to this group of five men would leave only one alive.

In his account of the battle, Private Harry O'Keefe, who had shipped-out with Oldfield on the *Kanowna,* reported that the squad of stretcher-bearers under Quirk had reached the area in the rear of the fighting between Clapham Junction and Hooge Tunnel when they were hit by a shell. Sergeant Robert Marrott of the 15th Field Ambulance in his report in relation to Private Arthur Joyce, wrote that despite not seeing the death, he saw Joyce's body and formed the opinion that, "he was caught by [a] piece of [high explosive] shell and killed instantly". Marrott goes on to say that Joyce was buried where he fell and his grave was marked by a cross bearing his number, name and unit.

In a report written by Lance Corporal Samuel Collis of the 15th Field Ambulance on 23 November 1917, he says Daly and Joyce were, "killed outright and [were] buried near the Tunnel [sic] Clapham Junction". Collis reported that Callon was wounded but died later and was buried at Boulogne. Reporting on Joyce's death, Private Charles James of the 15th Field Ambulance informed that he had seen Joyce's grave opposite the crater left by the shell that killed him and advised that, "Pte Oldfield [who] is now in England suffering shell shock" was one of the stretcher party and may have further information.

In his own very brief account in *Rattle of the Stumps* Oldfield recalled:-

"In the middle of one of the heavy barrages a Boche shell burst near our stretcher squad, killing three of my mates, while I was buried and lay unconscious".

At some point during the battle, or in its immediate aftermath, Oldfield was located and pulled out of the debris. He was taken to the casualty clearing station at the town of Poperinghe, west of Polygon Wood, and later transported to a military hospital in the city of Rouen, France. While undergoing treatment in the hospital, he developed the symptoms of 'shell-shock' and was invalided to England.

Now understood to be a form of post-traumatic stress disorder, the name 'shell-shock' was coined by military consulting psychologist Charles Myers in February 1915, to describe the new phenomenon. The term was used by authorities during World War 1 to describe post-battle symptoms which included extreme anxiety, inability to walk, night terrors, involuntary shaking, sensitivity to light and an inability to speak. The exposure of soldiers to unprecedented levels of high explosive artillery resulted in an escalation in cases of the affliction since the beginning of the war. The response of military authorities towards sufferers after initial scepticism and accusations of malingering, was to differentiate between casualties with direct concussion exposure as 'wounded' who would be eligible for 'wound stripe' recognition and pension coverage and those suffering from battlefield stress, designated as 'sick' and not eligible for recognition or pension. Oldfield was the former and in addition to his shell-shock his injuries included shrapnel wounds to the thigh, face and back as well as the initial partial-asphyxiation.

Due to the alarming volume of shell-shock cases after the Battle of the Somme in 1916, special psychiatric units were established to treat patients, providing rest and medical care in a calm environment. Four months into his own convalescence, Oldfield was able to offer further insight into the death of his friend and comrade Arthur Joyce in a report dated 24 January 1918. Many 'killed in action' reports from the time are bureaucratic and to-the-point yet Oldfield's account is tinged with sadness and warmth with the hope of providing comfort and assurance to Joyce's grieving family. From the 3rd Australian Auxiliary Hospital in Dartford, Oldfield wrote, "I wish to tell you that I was with this dear fellow on the day of the event...it will be very pleasing for you to know that Pte.A.A.A. Joyce died without suffering, for the blow was instantaneous". In an expression of consolation to the family he guaranteed that Joyce's body was "well cared for" and buried "quite safely and peacefully".

As was the case for the families of over 50,000 fallen Australian servicemen, the loss of 19-year-old Arthur Joyce was particularly devastating for his loved-ones and left a long-lasting bitterness. His father William James Joyce, the gardener of the beautiful harbour-side Elizabeth Bay House, refused to receive his son's Victory Medal or memorial plaque saying he did not require reminders that his son was killed in the war. Arthur Joyce's final resting place is at Polygon Wood where he was relocated from his battlefield burial to the New British Cemetery located on The Butte.

Lance Corporal Roy Quirk, the leader of the squad and Military Medal recipient from the 2nd Battle of Bullecourt in May 1917, is buried at the picturesque Lijssenthoek Military Cemetery at Poperinge, Belgium.

Unlike Joyce and Quirk, John Callon was not killed outright by the blast but died a day later of chest-penetrating shrapnel injuries and was laid to rest in the Wimereux Communal Cemetery north of Boulogne.

Polygon Wood was captured by Australian and British forces by mid-morning, taking stunned surrendering German soldiers prisoner and resisting desperate counterattacks, until fighting ceased in the evening. It was a complete, but costly victory with 9 square kilometres captured resulting in 5770 Australian casualties – of which Bert Oldfield was one.

THE A.I.F. CRICKET TEAM

Having sufficiently recovered from his physical and psychological wounds, Oldfield returned to duty when he was transferred to the Australian Imperial Force Kit Store in Hammersmith, London on 15 March 1918. Part of his role was the poignant duty of returning personal effects to the next-of-kin of servicemen who wouldn't be making the journey home. Managing the rows of storage shelves may have appealed to Oldfield's neat and orderly temperament.

Working out of the district of Hammersmith, he would have been aware of events across town with the reawakening of the game he loved. Charity matches to benefit war causes were scheduled for June and July 1918 between an England XI and a Dominions XI with two games at Lord's Cricket Ground and one at The Oval. A formidable home side boasting C.B. Fry, Percy Fender and Pelham 'Plum' Warner took on a Dominions side mainly composed of Australian and South African players. Springbok's Test player Herbie Taylor took to the field with Australians including Charlie Kelleway, Clarence 'Nip' Pellew, A.G. 'Johnnie' Moyes and Charlie Macartney. The Dominion's wicket-keeper was occasional New South Wales representative Ted Long who debuted in First-Class cricket back in 1911. Long was in his mid-30s and attained the rank of Captain during the war having worked with Oldfield at the 1st Dermatological Hospital in Cairo.

The three-match series was drawn with a wash-out at The Oval in the final match but proved to be a great success raising funds, attracting sizable crowds and confirming the public's appetite for the return of cricket once the hostilities finally came to an end. Playing for the local Wattle Cricket Club, Oldfield's cricketing profile remained modest, but by September 1918 he was promoted to Corporal just over three years after he walked to Victoria Barracks to enlist.

On 11 November 1918 the 'war to end all wars' came to an end after German Marshal Foch signed the armistice bringing into effect the cessation of four years of hostilities where up to 22 million people were killed – Bert Oldfield very nearly one of them. As one of the 165,000 Australian troops who survived the conflict, returning to family and friends at home would still be a long way off. It was estimated that it would take nine months to repatriate service personnel in England, France and Egypt back to Australia. The Australian Imperial Force command was faced with the dilemma of keeping a multitude of war-weary and homesick soldiers accommodated, occupied and entertained for months on end.

The Australian Corps Headquarters figured that sport was one of the best ways to keep the men active resulting in the formation of the A.I.F Sports Control Board in January 1919. Cricket had representation on the board in the form of Lieutenant-Colonel Jack Massie, the son of Test player Hugh, and 16-match New South Wales veteran himself. The giant left-arm fast-medium bowler would endure a series of injuries in battles at Gallipoli and the Western Front. Bullet and shrapnel wounds to his left shoulder and shoulder blade sustained at the Battle of Lone Pine in August 1915 would spell the end of his sporting career.

As early as December 1918 the Australian Board of Control for International Cricket had expressed interest in negotiating with its counterpart the Marylebone Cricket Club for a team of Australian servicemen to tour Great Britain. Early discussions had been promising until the extent of Australian cricketing talent that would be unavailable for selection became known. Players such as Charlie Macartney needed to return home to support his family after the death of his father, medical doctors Claude Tozer, Roy Park and Eric Barbour desired to return to their practices and war injuries prevented Jack Massie from participating. The Marylebone Cricket Club was unconvinced that a competitive side could be fielded and withdrew financial support for the initiative.

The auspices for the tour of an Australian Imperial Force Cricket Team now came under the direction of the A.I.F. Sports Control Board which organised team selection trials for April 1919. Oldfield was named in the 20-man trial for the team that would tour England and Scotland, but he was left disappointed when omitted from the side in favour of Ted Long. When the tour squad was formally announced he would have been dispirited when the team's back-up wicket-keeper was confirmed to be Balmain's Hampden 'Hammy' Love who had not even participated in the selection trials.

As the main team headed off on the tour, smaller A.I.F. teams played on Saturdays in competitions around London. If only for the love of the game and to keep himself occupied, Oldfield persisted in the subsidiary teams until an opportunity arose with a small tour of Oxford against university teams. As fate would often have it in the rise of Bert Oldfield, Hammy Love withdrew

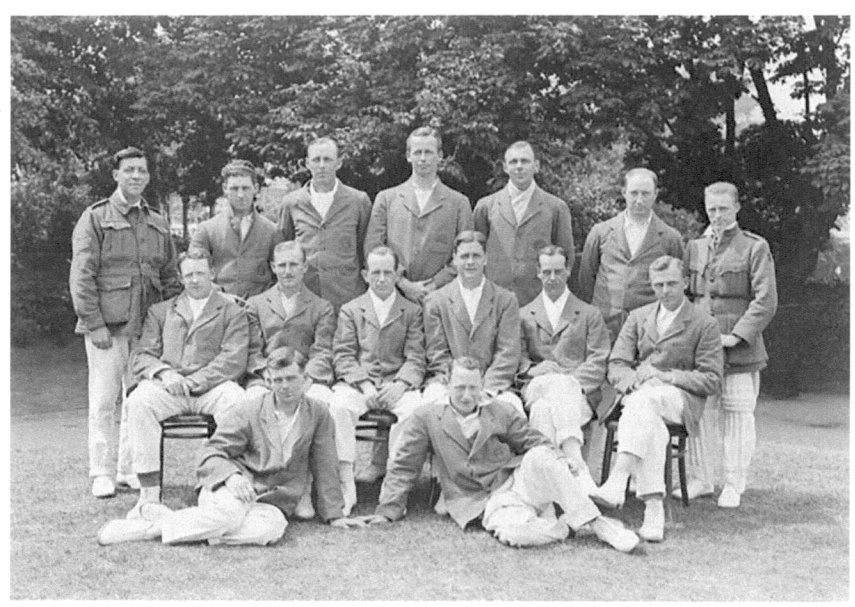

*Bert Oldfield (far right standing)
with the Australian Imperial Force Cricket Team.*

from the main side after the first match of the tour in mid-May to return to Australia. After his good performances in Oxford and with the opening of an understudy to Ted Long, Oldfield was elevated to the A.I.F. Cricket Team squad.

A consequence of Oldfield's ascent was a lasting admiration for Herbert Collins who had been on the cusp of national selection before the war and had assumed the captaincy of the A.I.F. team when previous leader Charlie Kelleway was dismissed by Field Marshal William Birdwood for being quarrelsome with the English locals. Oldfield said, "[Collins] had a sound knowledge of cricket; and just as important was a student of human nature…He endeared himself to each and every member of the team, and as a result we played and worked together in the best team spirit". He credited Collins with the development of future Test stars, all-rounder Jack

Gregory and batsman Johnny Taylor, as well as his own as a wicket-keeper. "Collins would sit on your bedside and talk over plans for a match that was to be played that day", Oldfield recalled.

The A.I.F team colours were not the traditional green and gold of Australian sport, but the cap and blazer were navy blue with the A.I.F. 'rising-sun' badge in gold and red embroidery, while the peak of the baggy-style cap was black. The tour rolled across England and into Scotland from May to early-September 1919 taking on county and representative sides in predominantly three-day matches. Of the 34 matches played, the A.I.F. won 15, drew 15 and lost only four. Twenty-eight of the matches were accredited First-Class status.

Oldfield played in 13 matches of the tour taking 16 catches and 10 stumpings while scoring 382 runs at 31.83 with a top score of 80 not out. Notably he participated in a 169-run 9th wicket partnership with Victorian batsman Carl Willis frustrating the Nottinghamshire bowling attack and personally scoring 65.

Towards the end of the England and Scotland tour, an approach was received from the government of South Africa which expressed interest in hosting the A.I.F. team for a six-week tour. South Africa had suffered significant losses in the war and the impact on domestic cricket in the country was immense with the deaths of Test representatives Frederick Cook, Reginald Hands, Bill Lundie, Claude Newberry, Arthur Ochse, Reggie Schwarz and Gordon White and a raft of other First-Class players.

On 23 September 1919 the team embarked for South Africa on the *Ascanius* from Devonport arriving in Cape Town on 13 October 1919. Across the late-Spring and into early summer, the A.I.F. team played the South African national side and the major provincial teams: Transvaal, Natal and Western Province twice each with a couple of games against college sides. The Australians remained

Bert Oldfield's trunk from the First World War which he brought home from the A.I.F tour.

undefeated on the tour winning eight matches and drawing two. The youthful understudy-keeper had effectively replaced Ted Long by the end of the tour with the latter only participating in one match. Oldfield had maintained a decent batting average with 220 runs at 31.42 with a highest score of 47 along with 15 catches and 4 stumpings.

On 13 December, the A.I.F. team boarded the *Aeneas* in Cape Town for the month-long voyage home. For some in the side, it would be a return home after almost five tumultuous years with the anticipation of reuniting with family and friends and resuming their pre-war lives. The arrival on Australian shores would not be the end of the A.I.F. team however, with plans afoot for matches against Sheffield Shield sides well underway while the team was in transit. Arriving in Adelaide on 2 January 1920, the A.I.F. would not be able to challenge the South Australian team which was in Melbourne on Sheffield Shield duties. The visitors expressed disappointment that the South Australian Cricket Association administrators did not take the opportunity to organise a match against a second XI side while they were there.

The A.I.F. team's chance to prove itself on home soil came on 16 January 1920, as they set foot on the hallowed turf of the Melbourne Cricket Ground. Herbie Collins surprised the Victorian team by sending them into bat. The Victorian team, boasting internationals Warwick Armstrong and Edgar Mayne and future Test players Jack Ryder and Ted McDonald, were utterly humbled in their first innings of 116 mainly through the pace of Jack Gregory (7 for 22). The A.I.F.'s Carl Willis belted 111 against his former teammates in the team's reply of 311, Oldfield batting at number 11 was 1 not out. Victoria did better in their second innings on a pitch now favouring spin. Oldfield took three of his 4 catches off leg-spinner Allie Lampard to add to his one catch from the first innings. Lampard, also a Victorian, took 7 for 99 against his former colleagues who were collectively dismissed for 270 leaving the A.I.F. 77 to win which they did with 6 wickets in hand.

The Woolloongabba ground in Brisbane hosted what was a typically rain-marred match in the subtropical city from 24 January. Facing certain defeat, the minnow Queensland team stubbornly held-on in their second innings until a storm arrived to force the draw. Oldfield was very active in the match bagging 5 catches and a stumping while letting through only 4 byes.

Oldfield's homecoming in Sydney after almost four-and-a-half years was to be momentous, not only would he be welcomed back into the warm embrace of his family, but he would play on the Sydney Cricket Ground – the city's premiere venue for the first time. His joy and relief may have been beset by uncertainty, not only in what he would do in his post-army life, but also in his cricketing career as he faced a New South Wales team with two wicket-keepers ahead of him in status – Andy Ratcliffe and Sammy Carter. Carter captained and kept for the formidable New South Wales side including fellow Test player Warren Bardsley and future internationals Hunter 'Stork' Hendry, Tommy Andrews, Arthur Mailey and Alan Kippax.

The A.I.F. batted first and posted 265 with all-rounder Jack Gregory starring with the bat this time – knocking 122 runs in typically aggressive fashion. New South Wales would slightly better the A.I.F. total with 279 in reply; Oldfield taking two catches and leaking 4 byes. In the second innings, captain Herbie Collins would avenge his first innings duck with a score of 129 while Jack Gregory produced a second hundred (102) in the match to take the A.I.F. to a commanding 395, setting New South Wales a mammoth 381 to chase. The home side collapsed to 178 handing the A.I.F victory by 112 runs. Despite snaring two catches in the final innings, Oldfield's offsider had a solid match taking 5 catches and a stumping. Seemingly, Sammy Carter remained unchallenged as Australia's premier wicket-keeper and it appeared that he would resume the position once Test cricket restarted.

The local leg of the A.I.F. tour heralded the emergence of a number future stars of Australian cricket that would make a considerable impact into the next decade. Jack Gregory averaging 75 with the bat and 14.65 with the ball confirmed him as a brilliant all-round prospect and Herbie Collins's solid batting, slow left-armers and leadership skills boded well for the future. Oldfield's batting had fallen away at home but his keeping was tidy with 13 catches and a stumping for the series.

With Carter and Ratcliffe ahead of him in the New South Wales wicket-keeping stakes and the more experienced Ted Long added to the mix, Oldfield may have wondered if his time with the A.I.F. team would be enough to push for higher honours, effectively in fourth position.

THE BAGGY GREEN

BERT OLDFIELD'S APPETITE FOR cricket was unabated, even after the exhausting experience of war service and 18 months of extensive touring with the Australian Imperial Force team. He was selected to represent the New South Wales Cricket Association along with Test player Charlie Macartney and state representative William Ives against the Interstate Administrative Railway Officers in a match at the Sydney Cricket Ground in February 1920.

After being discharged from the army on 10 March and awarded the 1914-1915 Star, the British War Medal and the Victory Medal for his service, Oldfield returned to work as a clerk, this time for the New South Wales railways. He immediately took-up where he left off – keeping for Glebe first grade and resuming club secretarial duties.

While his batting-slump continued on home soil, his wicket-keeping abilities continued to impress and he was rewarded with a First-Class debut for New South Wales against Queensland in the final match of the 1919-20 domestic season at the Sydney Cricket Ground. Of the debutant, the *Arrow* newspaper of 9 April 1920 reported, "W.A. Oldfield, as wicketkeeper, was A1. He is quite First-Class, very keen and alert and a trier [sic]. We did not see him at his best with the bat, though he got to 14 and then played one on to the sticks". Oldfield took a pair of catches and effected a pair of stumpings in the match.

During the winter of 1920, Oldfield entered into lifelong membership of the fraternal society, the Masonic Lodge initiated into Sydney's Arcadia No.117 chapter on 11 June 1920. Its origins shrouded in mystery, The Lodge transformed over the centuries from a trade union of Middle Age stone masons to a secretive pantheistic order. Freemasonry arrived on Australian shores with the First Fleet, the early lodges predominantly military. A civilian lodge was established in 1820 with the United Grand Lodge of New South Wales founded in 1888. In early-20th century Australia, membership of the Masonic Lodge was invariably sought by Protestant men such as Oldfield, as a two-century-old Papal Bull against Roman Catholic association with Freemasonry remained in effect with the threat of excommunication.

༄

The resumption of the venerated Anglo-Australian cricketing contest 'The Ashes' in the Australian summer of 1920-21 inspired growing selection conjecture in the Autumn of 1920. In an assessment of the previous season's form and future prospects in *Smith's Weekly* of 1 May, Oldfield was ranked as the second wicket-keeper in New South Wales behind Sammy Carter. Victorian keeper Bill 'Barlow' Carkeek, who was the incumbent Australian keeper after playing in the 1912 Test tri-series against England and South Africa, was in his early-40s and had not resumed his playing career after the war.

Speculation in the *Sydney Morning Herald* of 7 July, nominated Carter as the lead gloveman with New South Wales's Oldfield and

Ratcliffe on even-footing ahead of Victoria's Jack Ellis and South Australia's Julius Schultz.

After playing warm-up matches with Glebe in September 1920, Oldfield was selected for a New South Wales trial match at the Sydney Cricket Ground for the Herbie Collins XI against the Charlie Macartney XI. After lanky seamer Stork Hendry ripped through the Collins XI's top-order, Oldfield impressed with the bat scoring 51 not out rescuing the innings with A.I.F. teammate Johnny Taylor from 7/37 to reach 7/159 at stumps. The next weekend he pushed on to 76 when he became one of Hendry's four victims before the Collins team was dismissed for 224 – Taylor was not out on 126.

In the Macartney XI's reply, Oldfield impressed with two stumpings off future wicket-taking partner Arthur Mailey's leg-breaks. So remarkable was his performance that selectors chose him over Sammy Carter for the upcoming practice matches against the English tourists. Oldfield's keeping technique up to the stumps was praised in the press and a critic in the *Referee* of 3 November 1920 argued that Oldfield had edged ahead of Carter as preferred Australian keeper due to his superior batsmanship.

The practice matches against England in late-November enjoyed fine weather, a great S.C.G. pitch and overwhelming support from the public with eager, cricket-starved crowds of around 34,000 spectators in attendance. The England team brought to Australian shores a remarkable array of talent after almost a decade's absence. The touring party included the likes of Jack Hobbs, 'Patsy' Hendren, Frank Woolley, Johnny Douglas, Percy Fender and Wilfred Rhodes.

Oldfield remained in the selectors' favour ahead of Carter and Ratcliffe when he was picked to make his Sheffield Shield debut against South Australia at the Sydney Cricket Ground on 3 December 1920. He would take a backseat however, as he witnessed the New South Wales batsmen amass a colossal first innings score of 802. Glebe teammates Warren Bardsley and Charles Kelleway made 235 and 168 respectively supported by James Bogle 103, Johnny Taylor 95 and Stork Hendry with 82. Despite the clobbering, the game ended in a draw after South Australia's reply of 191 and 0/6 with both sides agreeing to call it off in the days of timeless matches.

As if writing a fairytale, the Australian selectors chose Oldfield to make his Test debut at his home ground, in an Ashes series, in what would be a significant Test match – almost 8-and-a-half years since the last one was played at The Oval in 1912. Living back in the family home at 'Cotswold' in Glebe Point, Oldfield recalled:-

"We were at our evening meal when Charlie Kelleway....called and told the good news. My mother, whose face was wreathed in smiles, rushed back into the dining room and the members of the family wondered what it was all about. After a while she came over and kissed me and loudly whispered: 'How wonderful, Bertie, you've been picked for the First Test!' I was so excited I could not finish my meal....I saw myself wearing the much-coveted green cap bearing the Australian coat of arms and walking out onto the field in the select company of such celebrities as Noble, Armstrong, Macartney, Kellaway [sic], Bardsley, Cotter, Ransford and others whose skill had won them international fame".

He would be one of seven debutants along with Herbie Collins, Jack Gregory, Johnny Taylor, Nip Pellew, Jack Ryder and Arthur Mailey. Out of the quartet of veterans returning to the Test arena, Warwick 'The Big Ship' Armstrong was appointed to the captaincy over Bardsley, Kelleway and Macartney. The England team would have the slight edge on Australia in terms of experience with seasoned players returning including Douglas, Hearne, Woolley, Rhodes and the brilliant Hobbs. Despite the practice matches in Sydney, the visitors may have still been slightly underdone after a period in quarantine due to a typhus outbreak onboard their voyage to Australia.

Oldfield posed for the team photograph in his new Baggy Green cap and green blazer with gold piping prior to the Test match – his face barely containing his excitement. On 17 December 1920, the Sydney Cricket Ground was bursting at the seams, with its green corrugated-iron roofed stands adorned with flags, turrets and domed towers drenched in sunlight. Captain Armstrong won the toss and chose to bat, while most Australian batsmen made starts, only Herbie Collins capitalised with 70 on debut. Oldfield was dismissed for only 7 coming-in at number 10 in

Bert Oldfield (standing far left) posing with the Australian Cricket Team before his debut Test.

the order – the score 267. In reply, England made a poor start to the series being dismissed for 190. Arthur Mailey and Oldfield took the first of many combined Test wickets tempting England captain Johnny Douglas out of his crease to find his bails smartly dislodged for 21. Centuries from Collins (104) and Armstrong (158) took Australia to a commanding lead in the second innings with a total of 581. Gregory, Mailey and Kelleway took three wickets each in the quelling of the English second innings of 281 resulting in an Australian victory by 344. Oldfield caught one of Gregory's offerings and added another victim to the stumping tally off Mailey.

Australia's dominance continued in the second Test at the Melbourne Cricket Ground as Oldfield scored 24 of the team's 499. Charlie Macartney had been replaced in the batting order by Victorian Dr Roy Park who was famously dismissed for a golden duck – his wife having missed his entire Test batting career when she leaned over to pick up a dropped ball of wool. England failed to scale Australia's total in two attempts resulting in an innings and 91-run defeat. Oldfield's work was solid again with a stumping in the first innings and a caught-behind off his captain in the second while only allowing 3 byes through.

Another Collin's century (162) in the third Test at the Adelaide Oval saw the Australians make a first innings score of 354 with Oldfield knocking his maiden Test half-century (50). In a high-scoring match, Australia would prevail by 119 runs, but despite Oldfield featuring in two Mailey stumpings in each innings and reportedly playing bravely with two broken fingers, his position in the team was being questioned in some quarters.

Two days prior to the fourth Test in Melbourne, Australian Board of Control secretary Sydney Smith announced that Oldfield would be replaced by 42-year-old Sammy Carter in the squad.

The *Daily Telegraph* of 9 February 1921 declared, "[m]any people, including prominent players, incline to the emphatic belief that Carter is still the best 'knight of the gloves' in Australia; that he should throughout have been Australia's first keeper" while praising Oldfield as a "batsman of great promise". Australia went-on to win the next two Tests, clean-sweeping England 5-nil and retaining the coveted Ashes.

The stinging disappointment of being dropped from the Test side would be short-lived with an offer from the Board of Control to be back-up keeper for the Ashes tour of England starting in May 1921. Oldfield's shortened debut Test series resulted in 107 runs at 21.40 with two catches, five stumpings and 20 byes in three matches.

UNDERTAKER'S UNDERSTUDY

THE 1920-21 FIRST-CLASS CRICKET season had barely concluded before it was time to prepare for the voyage to England. On the first day of March 1921, the Glebe District Cricket Club held a farewell for the club's tourists Warren Bardsley and Bert Oldfield at the Glebe Town Hall. The gathering was attended by around 200 people including Sammy Carter who had regained his position as Test keeper and the club's other international Charles Kelleway who had withdrawn from the Ashes tour.

An undertaker by trade, the warmly-received Carter addressed the gathering and confirmed that rumours of tension between himself and Oldfield were erroneous and regretted that they had been given the time of day. Carter declared that he and his young colleague were "the best of friends" and that he would impart his knowledge with him at every opportunity. He also expressed his sadness over the death of Glebe's Albert 'Tibby' Cotter who had died in the charge of the Light Horse at Beersheba in 1917, recalling his experiences as a state and Test teammate. Oldfield and Bardsley were presented with travel bags and money which they promptly returned for the benefit of the club.

Despite the kind gesture, the diminutive keeper may have been short of funds at the time after being the victim of an alleged confidence trickster. In February 1921, Oldfield had met a man named Ronald Bourne who had been discussing business opportunities with the rising cricket star confiding that he had been considering becoming a trade agent importing goods from France. The 36-year-old Bourne advised Oldfield that he had good connections in trade with England and suggested he would be a good fit to manage a firm he was associated with on an annual salary of £600 ($49,500). After further negotiations, Bourne said he was heading to do business in Melbourne and offered to convert cash for gold on his behalf. Oldfield obliged by handing Bourne £260 ($21,400) after withdrawing it from a bank in Sydney's Martin Place. Rather than going to Melbourne, Bourne went on a drinking bender instead in the Blue Mountains outside Sydney. He was arrested by New South Wales police detectives in Katoomba, appeared before Central Police Court on 4 March 1921 on the charge of false pretences and was remanded in custody. After a week the matter went to trial but Bourne was able to convince the jury that he had no guilty intent in regards to Oldfield's money but made an unfortunate decision and was subsequently acquitted of the charge. A majority of the rather substantial sum was returned to its rightful owner.

Despite his surprising acquittal, Ronald Bourne would be sentenced to two-years hard labour in 1926 for again obtaining money by means of false pretence in an elaborate scheme where he convinced an unwitting woman that he was a British Secret Service agent.

With court testimony behind him and the bulk of his money returned, touring life resumed for Oldfield with a journey across to the other side of the continent for matches against a Goldfields

XV at Kalgoorlie and the Western Australia team at Perth before embarking to England in late March 1921. The month-long voyage was not kind to the 15th Australian touring team with Warren Bardsley arriving in England with a dose of ptomaine poisoning, Johnny Taylor and Stork Hendry suffering colds and Oldfield having sustained an arm injury after a fall on the boat. In addition to sickness and injury the wet weather conspired to hamper preparations. In spite of the travails that confronted the motley-troupe of antipodean cricketers, 'Armstrong's Australians' would utterly demoralise English cricket in their six-months abroad.

In 39 matches, the Australian team won 23 (including 3 Tests), drew 14 and looked like they were going to be undefeated until surprising late losses to an England XI at Eastbourne and C.I. Thornton's XI in the final match at Scarborough. The 42-year-old, 21-stone (133 kilogram) captain Warwick 'The Big Ship' Armstrong

The 1921 Australian Cricket Team captained by Warwick Armstrong. Bert Oldfield is seated on the ground (right), Hanson 'Sammy' Carter is seated behind his left shoulder.

would unknowingly end his Test career with a fine all-round performance of 1213 First-Class tour runs at 41.82 and topping the averages with his leg-spinners with 100 wickets at 14.44 apiece. Veteran batsmen Charlie Macartney and Warren Bardsley both exceeded 2000 tour runs at 59.41 and 54.18 respectively, however the decisive factor in Australia's success would be the fast bowling pairing of Jack Gregory and Ted McDonald. Tasmanian-born McDonald took 138 First-Class wickets at 16.55 with his graceful action while Gregory took 116 at 16.58 with his kangaroo hop-style deliveries while contributing 1135 with the bat at 36.61.

On Friday 29 July 1920, Freemasons from 14 Masonic Lodges around southern England held a reception for their Australian cricketing brothers at Southend, outside London. Oldfield, the fledgling Mason was joined by Charlie Macartney, Arthur Mailey and team manager Sydney Smith who spoke about the history of Australian Freemasonry for the gathering. The emergent wicket-keeper continued to develop close ties with fellow Freemasons over the ensuing years.

Having been relegated to watching Sammy Carter keep from the stands for most of the Ashes series, Oldfield got to play his only Test of the series in the final rain-plagued dead rubber at The Oval in mid-August. While taking a caught-behind off McDonald he managed to improve his average with 28 not out in Australia's only innings. Oldfield kept wicket in 18 tour matches (one more than Carter) scoring 355 runs at 23.80, taking 33 catches and effecting 24 stumpings. Carter in comparison took 26 catches while stumping 12 and scoring 355 runs at 20.88. The younger understudy also scored his maiden First-Class century against Warwickshire with 123 batting at number 10.

The victorious Australians boarded the *Balmoral Castle* for the month-long Atlantic voyage down to South Africa for a six-Test tour arriving in Cape Town in October 1921. 'Armstrong's Australians' now became the team of Herbie Collins after the 'Big Ship' contracted malaria during the voyage, which in addition to leg injuries, put an earlier end to his career than anticipated – but he stayed-on with the tour to provide moral support.

In October, the team played tour matches against Transvaal in Johannesburg and Natal in Durban – beating both comfortably. Seniority ensured Sammy Carter got the nod to keep in the first Test against South Africa in Durban which ended in a draw. Oldfield was picked for the second Test at the Old Wanderer's ground in Johannesburg where he was bowled for 2 but took a gutsy stumping keeping up to fast-medium pacer Jack Ryder on the coir matting wicket. Despite 203 to captain Collins and Gregory's maiden Test century of 119, poor light saw the Test fizzle-out to a draw. Back in Cape Town, Western Province provided no obstacle in the tour match at Newlands. With the return of Carter in the Test match at the same venue South Africa was defeated by 10 wickets to hand Australia victory in the series.

The all-conquering team returned to Australia prior to Christmas 1921 and were warmly welcomed upon arrival in Adelaide by South Australian Cricket Association president Mostyn Evan. There being no Test series over the Australian season, the interstate Sheffield Shield competition became the focus of the summer. Exhausted New South Wales players Oldfield and Macartney, who had not been home for eight months, headed back to Sydney foregoing the chance to play in the Shield match against Victoria in Melbourne starting on Christmas Eve. In a feat of endurance Collins, Andrews, Taylor, Gregory, Carter, Hendry and Mailey backed-up from the tour to spend Christmas away from home to play even more cricket.

As Oldfield returned to 'Cotswold' to enjoy Christmas with his family and share stories of his travels, a further development in Melbourne made the contest for New South Wales wicket-keeper even more congested with Balmain (and briefly A.I.F.) gloveman Hammy Love scoring 102, playing as a batsman at number 3 for New South Wales. A critic in the *Arrow* newspaper of 30 December 1921, suggested Love, "such a fine wicket-keeper as he is" had the edge over Carter, Ratcliffe and Oldfield due to his superior batsmanship.

Initially named in the New South Wales squad for the 7 January 1922 match against South Australia at the Sydney Cricket Ground, Oldfield was withdrawn to be rested. Carter and Love having also been rested and with Ratcliffe unavailable, Waverley firsts keeper Harry Savage was plucked from Sydney Grade Cricket for his only First-Class appearance. Hendry, Andrews and Mailey were the only regulars in the team which still defeated the Croweaters, captained by future Test batsman Victor Richardson.

The selectors, figuring they needed to keep their powder dry for the final match against Victoria, ordered Tuesday and Thursday afternoon practices at the Sydney Cricket Ground for the full-strength squad including Collins, Macartney, Bardsley, Gregory and Oldfield. Careful preparation did not save the worn-out New South Wales batting order from the devastating pace of Ted McDonald however. The silken McDonald took 11 wickets in the match with 8 for 84 in the final innings, six of which were bowled. Winning by 154 runs in enemy territory, Victoria headed south taking the Sheffield Shield home with them. As the cricket petered-out at the end of another season, Oldfield returned to grade cricket for Glebe and had a late highlight taking 5 catches in the Frank Iredale benefit match at the Sydney Cricket Ground.

The Australian Board of Control announced that the 1921 tour to England and South Africa had raised an amazing £17,000

($1,430,000) which would be shared between the players and the state boards. Each player would receive £300 ($25,000) bonus on top of £400 ($33,600) for the England tour and £88 ($7400) for the South African leg. After a season of mixed fortunes in cricketing terms, the tired 27-year-old was going to take time out to reflect and consider how to best use his hard-earned windfall into making a future for himself.

In an interview in the *Referee* newspaper of 15 February 1922 under the headline 'LEAVING FOR ENGLAND W.A. Oldfield Going on a Health Trip', he said the journey was primarily for a, "good sea and rest change," and that he had, "not been feeling at his top in health after the strenuous cricket campaign". Oldfield admitted to the paper that "[w]hen he returned from the war he suffered a good deal with his nerves and he has been in the vortex of The Ashes cricket, he has not had a chance to relax". Responding to gossip that he would be staying in England permanently possibly to pursue a career in county cricket, Oldfield assured that he was also going to investigate business interests while away and expressed hope he would, "come back to Australia feeling thoroughly fit".

The rumours about the nature of Oldfield's departure sparked increasing speculation regarding other prominent players like Herbie Collins, Warren Bardsley and Edgar Mayne making lucrative careers in professional cricket in England's Lancashire League rather than having to juggle a regular career with semi-professional cricket in Australia. Ultimately, defection into the English system came from unexpected quarters with bowler Ted McDonald walking away from his fledgling 11-Test career in the interests of ensuring financial security.

While holidaying in England, Oldfield could not resist the urge to don the keeping gloves. He played in a couple of matches which included an invitation to keep-wicket for the House of

Commons against the House of Lord's on June 15 1922. To the relief of the cricketing community in Australia, reports spread of Oldfield's homecoming. Arriving in Fremantle with crates of sporting equipment, he announced in the *Evening News* of 5 August 1922 that he was going to open a sports depot in Sydney and had brought back a design for a wicket-keeping glove which would be locally-manufactured.

Returning to Sydney, he registered the trademark 'W.A.Oldfield Pty Ltd' and launched the W.A. Oldfield's Sports Depot at 54 Hunter Street in Sydney's central business district advertising the 'Largest stock, Lowest prices, Repairs of all kinds' in the city's newspapers. Monday 28 August 1922 was the opening day for the store with the new proprietor assuring the public that all items were "personally selected" by him. Not only would the sports depot stock imported goods but Oldfield entered partnerships with Australian manufacturers Stokes McGown Ltd to produce his signature range of wicket-keeping gloves and would add his endorsement to bats made by the Sykes manufacturer.

Herbert Stanley Geldard, a hero in the Battle of Polygon Wood back in 1917 who was awarded the Military Cross in recognition of his leadership as a lieutenant in the capture of The Butte, joined Oldfield briefly as a partner in the sports store until the pair dissolved by mutual consent in 1925. Geldard would later establish a long-running business partnership with Oldfield's state and Test teammate Alan Kippax as a part of his consortium, the New South Wales Sports Store in Sydney's Martin Place.

The annually-published 'Oldfield's Sports Manual' focussed on the popular sports of cricket, golf and tennis and contained articles written by Oldfield on wicket-keeping and teammate Charlie Macartney on batting technique. Additional contributions to the manual included golfer Sam Richardson and Australasian and Wimbledon doubles champion James Anderson on tennis. Oldfield went on to publish regular advice pamphlets and print his own brand of cricket scorebooks.

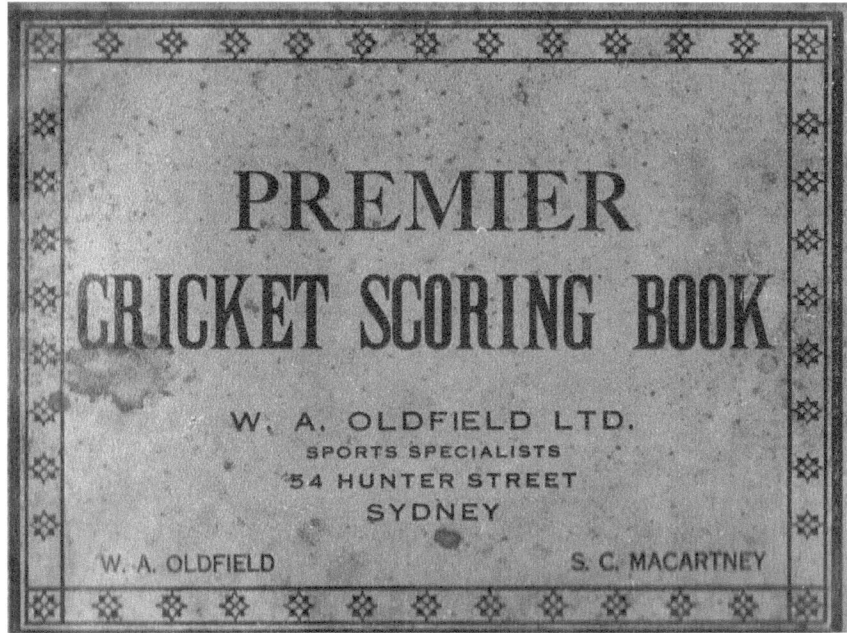

The W.A. Oldfield Premier Cricket Scorebook.

Rejuvenated by his sojourn to England and excited by his new business venture, Oldfield started the 1922-23 season with the Glebe club in another year where Sheffield Shield would be the main event of the summer with no international touring side coming to Australia. Oldfield's rising status still seemed to be causing resentment with the 'old-boys' network after former Australia captain Monty Noble came out in the pre-season press favouring his former Test and state teammate Sammy Carter, now 44, as the best gloveman in the country.

The New South Wales selectors did not concur with the likes of Noble, selecting Oldfield as keeper for the first Shield game against South Australia in Adelaide. The royal blues inflicted another pounding on the hapless Croweaters with an innings and 310-run victory. The New South Wales first innings of 786 boasted four centurions including Oldfield's 118 – his first on home soil. He was also active behind the stumps with three catches and two Mailey stumpings.

Oldfield finished the 1922-23 domestic season with 22 catches, 15 stumpings and a batting average of 21.27 in nine games. He would also complete his ascension as the premier wicket-keeper in New South Wales, if not the country, with Andy Ratcliffe relegated to reserve state keeper, Hammy Love moving to Victoria and Sammy Carter retiring to the ranks of Sydney Grade Cricket.

THE ROARING 20S

As **Australia's leading gloveman,** Bert Oldfield's technique and style would be emulated by a generation of young wicket-keepers and become the training standard for decades. Fastidiously neat with tailored playing gear, he favoured the use of large 'gauntlet' gloves in preference to streamlined styles. Eucalyptus oil was used to keep the leather conditioned.

To protect his hands, finger joints were bound with adhesive tape and covered with two pairs of chamois inner-gloves fastened with an elastic band around the wrist. At the end of a hard-day behind the stumps, Oldfield recommended soaking hands in warm water to keep them supple and apply embrocation if required.

Imitating his predecessor Sammy Carter, the basic Oldfield wicket-keeping stance would not find a welcome place in contemporary instruction manuals. In contrast to the modern practice of crouching with elbows between the knees, open palms facing the bowler and fingertips touching the ground; his elbows were tucked into his waist with gloves facing inward at around bail height.

Bert Oldfield keeping wicket for New South Wales in the 1920s.

Oldfield's stumping technique was best-practice: body behind the line of the ball, gloves accepting the delivery (not grabbing) and removing the bails with swift arm movement. His reception of throws from the outfield would be peculiar to modern observers, as he invariably squatted behind the stumps, eyes close to bail-level to judge the ball's trajectory with gloves splayed open.

Equally important to his wicket-keeping skills was his on-field conduct, which was the subject of growing admiration.

Anointed the nickname 'Cracker' by his teammates, Oldfield was constantly the centre of attention – the drummer in the band – cheerily injecting himself in all aspects of the play. When making a stumping, he would not demolish the stumps, but affect the minimal amount of disturbance possible to the 'furniture' – often satisfied with dislodging one bail in achieving the task. Opponents were guaranteed a warm congratulation from the little keeper when achieving a batting milestone and be granted polite gloved-applause from behind the wicket for a well-timed boundary.

Oldfield took time away from his burgeoning city sports business to venture beyond the Great Dividing Range for a promotional and speaking tour of New South Wales regional cities and towns in the winter of 1923. Members of local cricket associations in centres like Lithgow, Mudgee, Goulburn, Bathurst, Wagga and Forbes listened to his recollections of experiences as a Test player and advice for up-and-comers. Oldfield told of the New South Wales Cricket Association's plans to foster cricket in the bush and get teams to Sydney in order to identify talent. The budding businessman also brought samples of his new range of signature keeping gloves hot off the production line.

Warren Bardsley's surprise defection from the Glebe club down the Parramatta Road to the neighbouring Western Suburbs club resulted in Oldfield being handed the captaincy of the firsts a decade after joining the club. After the obligatory intrastate trial matches and a trip to Newcastle with an Arthur Mailey XI, Oldfield's appointment as state wicket-keeper was now a *fait accompli* for New South Wales selectors Dr Leslie Poidevin, Charlie Macartney and Warren Bardsley for another non-Test domestic season. The emergence of talented young Victorians like Bill Ponsford and Bill Woodfull and solid performances from old hands like Edgar Mayne saw the southern state clean-sweep the Sheffield Shield to retain it for another year. Oldfield equal-topped the First-Class dismissals ladder with South Australian keeper Bert Ambler with 10 catches and 9 stumpings each. In February and March of 1924, New South Wales toured New Zealand to play provincial teams and the New Zealand national side twice in non-Test status matches in Christchurch and Wellington. Oldfield played all 6 games of the tour, telling the *Referee* upon his return that he was quite hopeful for cricket in New Zealand remarking that it, "was a very fine trip, and we enjoyed it very much".

Soon after his return to Australia, Oldfield's burgeoning success in the business and sporting world led to him purchasing a home at 18 Provincial Road, Lindfield on Sydney's Upper North Shore for his parents, siblings and himself to reside. After a decade with his beloved Glebe club and soon after being appointed captain of the first-grade team, he was forced to resign his services. Now living within the Gordon cricket district catchment area, he joined the local club based at Chatswood Oval. The new move would also necessitate a change in commute for the sportsman-cum-businessman including a daily train ride from Lindfield Railway Station down the North Shore line to Milsons Point station and a ferry ride across the harbour from Milsons Point wharf to Circular Quay with a short walk to his Hunter Street business premises. A newly-proposed bridge across the harbour linking the North Shore to the city would provide an additional commuting option in the future.

Illness threatened to thwart the Australian keeper's 1924-25 Ashes preparations after he was admitted to the Darcross Private Hospital in Killara with appendicitis, going under the knife on the night of 27 August 1924. Oldfield expressed hope he would only be out of action for a fortnight, but was eventually released on 17 September. Donning the maroon cap of the Gordon club would not come immediately but fresh air and convalescence for two weeks in rural Taree would take priority. Oldfield's absence offered Sammy Carter a momentary comeback to the New South Wales team for an October match against an Australian XI made up of the remaining state teams.

In early-November 1924, Oldfield returned to cricket at the Sydney Cricket Ground for the New South Wales First XI match against the Second XI. Resuming his keeping duties with no ill-effects, the game was marred by a thief ransacking the Members Pavilion dressing rooms and stealing £18 worth of cash and jewellery with Oldfield personally having £2 stolen. No longer having to endure press speculation into his position on the nation's wicket-keeping pecking order, he added another string to his bow. Oldfield's first foray into radio broadcasting came on the eve of the Test series with his 15-minute cricket segments on the Australian Broadcasting Commission's Sydney station 2BL, nightly from 7:30pm.

Excitement continued to grow for the upcoming Ashes series after an almost three-year hiatus of Test cricket after the post-war resumption of the international game. Four years after his Test debut, Oldfield had only five appearances to boast of and would value every opportunity to build on the tally. A tour match against the Marylebone Cricket Club and a Sheffield Shield game against South Australia heralded his full recovery and confirmed his fitness for national duties in the lead-up to the Tests.

The first Test of the 1924-25 Ashes at the Sydney Cricket Ground saw a high-scoring contest with each side containing three centurions, including Bill Ponsford (110) on debut for Australia and the world's greatest batsman England's Jack Hobbs showing ominous form with his score of 115. Australia would eventually prevail with a 193 run victory despite an 11 wicket haul from England's nagging medium pacer Maurice Tate.

Australia took the winning tally to 2-nil in the second Test at the Melbourne Cricket Ground starting New Years Day 1925. Bill Ponsford scored his second century in as many Tests with 128 as the green caps amassed a total of 600. Despite their openers Jack Hobbs scoring 154 and Herbert Sutcliffe 176 and 127, England could not prevail in a Test that would finally end on its seventh day with the tourists 81 runs in arrears.

Jack Hobbs completed his hat-trick of centuries in another gruelling seven-day third Test match at the Adelaide Oval. It would be Jack Ryder's turn to join the centurions with 201 not out in the first innings of Australia's 11 run win, wrapping up the series and retaining the Ashes.

Back at the Melbourne Cricket Ground for the fourth Test, Oldfield achieved the milestone of five dismissals in England's only innings – one caught and four stumped. Displaying his courage and deft skills, two stumpings were off fast-medium pacers in Charlie Kelleway and Jack Ryder with the other two off Arthur Mailey's turners. Oldfield considered the legside stumping of Hobbs off Ryder to be his best of all. This Test would be England's only bright spot of the series with a win by an innings and 29 runs.

After four Tests, England's 42-year-old batting genius Jack Hobbs had compiled 560 runs at an average of 80 in each innings and the stage was set for him to capitalise again in the fifth Test at the Sydney Cricket Ground with Australia only making a modest total of 295 in their first innings. What would happen next would become a cherished memory for Oldfield mirroring his dismissal of Syd Gregory almost a decade prior on Wentworth Park before the war.

Oldfield's favourite stumping, catching Jack Hobbs out of his crease.

Hobbs opened the batting and was taking strike at the Randwick End, Jack Gregory stood tall at the end of his mark at the Paddington End with a gleaming new ball in hand. Oldfield could clearly recall the beautiful ground bathed in sunlight and a north-east wind pushing over Gregory's shoulder. As Gregory bowled the first couple of deliveries, the keeper noticed the breeze forcing the ball to tail down Hobbs's leg side, while the third ball stayed on a straight trajectory. Like the first two balls, the fourth ball was picked-up by the gust making it pitch outside the leg stump which lured Hobbs into attempting a leg-glance and nicking an edge. Oldfield recalled that he had, "anticipated its course by covering a greater distance, and as soon as I heard the snick I stretched my arms full length while in my stride, probably four or five yards wide of the wicket, which certainly thrilled me and bought the spectators as a man to their feet".

A photograph taken at that precise moment captures the tension vividly. Watched by thousands in the background on the Sydney Cricket Ground hill, a wrong-footed Hobbs twists his head to the left to witness the fate of the ball. Captain Collins in the gully and Kelleway and Mailey in the slips cordon are caught in early reaction at Oldfield, arms fully-stretched face inclined upward into the early-afternoon sunlight. Jack Ryder at first slip apparently misses the event seemingly preoccupied with the batsman. Oldfield remembered, "[t]he roar of the crowd brought

Oldfield's favourite catch of his career.
Snaring England's Jack Hobbs down the leg side.

home for me the sensation of the catch. There was no describing my delight at the achievement in dismissing such a redoubtable batsman. I can still see Gregory continuing his run down the wicket to greet me with a smile, while Hobbs quietly left the scene, no doubt amazed by the suddenness of it all".

Australia went on to win the final Test with an emphatic 4-1 result in the series. Oldfield had finally strung a full Test series together and demonstrated a distinct improvement in his batting form. He scored 273 runs at an average of 39 with a high score of 65 not out. Despite allowing 35 byes to slip over the series he took nine catches and eight stumpings, some of the dismissals of the series among the highlights of his career.

Oldfield spent the winter of 1925 pouring his energies into his sports depot. Cautious after his previous negative encounter of the business world, he went into partnership with his friend, teammate and Freemason, Charlie Macartney. Oldfield also appointed his brother-in-law Anton 'Tony' Sattler, who was wed to his sister Lyle, as manager of the store. With cricket taking him interstate and overseas for months-on-end, a trusted associate overseeing the business would be invaluable for Oldfield's peace-of-mind. Sadly his father John would not get to enjoy the family's move to the North Shore for very long, dying at home at the Provincial Road property on 29 August 1925, aged 72.

Oldfield continued his expanding schedule of public speaking engagements, including a visit to his old stomping ground in Sydney's Inner-West by addressing the annual general meeting of the Western Suburbs Churches Cricket Union and donating a bat he had brought back from England for fundraising purposes.

A studio portrait of Bert Oldfield in the mid-1920s.

In mid-September the Mailey-Oldfield duo went on a road trip to the Riverina town of West Wyalong to play in a benefit match for local cricketer Phil King who had sustained a severe eye injury during a match the previous season. Playing the nearby town of Forbes, the West Wyalong top-order collapsed but Oldfield steadied the ship with 102, getting the local team to 245. Forbes struggled in reply with Mailey in top form bagging 6 for 42 to have the visitors all out for 70. Oldfield was busy behind the wicket with a catch and three stumpings. Between the match and a benefit dance at the Masonic Hall that evening, around £80 ($6700) was raised for the injured local cricketer.

At the commencement of the 1925-26 season, the Gordon club enjoyed the services of Charlie Macartney, Oldfield and fellow Glebe import Charles Kelleway until state honours called them away. The New South Wales keeper came second on the First-Class dismissals list to Victoria's Jack Ellis who revelled in the stumping opportunities afforded to him by the finger spinning partnership of Bert Ironmonger and Don Blackie. Unusually, Oldfield's batting was the stand-out aspect of his game with an average of 50 and a high score of 129. In another non-Test year, the royal blues took back the Sheffield Shield from Victoria with a four-match clean-sweep of the season.

A sixteen-man squad was selected in February for the 1926 Ashes tour of England. The selectors favoured experience over youth with Collins, Bardsley, Andrews, Ryder, Taylor, Hendry, Macartney and Mailey making what would be their final campaigns in the Old Country. South Australian all-rounder Arthur Richardson and New South Wales quick Sam Everett would get their first and only England tour, as would reserve keeper, Jack Ellis.

Forming the basis of the future Test team were Oldfield, New Zealand-born Clarrie Grimmett and Victorian batting aces Bill Ponsford and Bill Woodfull on their first trips. Considered unfortunate to miss-out on the tour were rookie batsmen Alan Kippax and Victor Richardson and veteran all-rounder Charlie Kelleway, of whom many felt was omitted from the touring squad due to politics.

A wet English summer, 3-day Test matches, illness and discontent conspired to thwart the touring Australian Cricket Team. After four drawn games it was decided that the fifth Test at The Oval in London would be timeless to force a series result. A 172 opening partnership between Hobbs (100) and Sutcliffe (161) in England's second innings total of 436 decided Australia's fate as they were bowled-out 289 runs short and the Ashes were lost.

The 1926 Ashes tour ended with the usual speculation about Australian players being tempted by the opportunity to play cricket professionally in England with Bill Ponsford confirming rumours saying that he was indeed interested in playing in the Blackpool League if he could, "induce his wife to settle in England". A front-page exposé in the *Truth* of 7 November 1926, authored by the spurned Australian cricketer Charlie Kelleway, aimed to shed light on Ponsford's surprising revelation. Kelleway had inside information that comradeship and team spirit had broken down to the point that even the new players felt demoralised, "some of whom were entirely fed up by the time the tour had commenced in earnest". Kelleway continued to opine that "[i]t was a crying shame that they should have been allowed to get into this frame of mind- and so early too". Kelleway reserved particular criticism for tour manager Sydney Smith who he blamed for allowing the team to devolve into multiple cliques and indulging in extravagances such as retaining a personal typist on the tour. He also accused Herbie Collins (whom he was dumped in favour of as captain of the A.I.F. team a decade prior) of attending the horse races when recovering from injury in preference to his duties as a selector.

It is unknown which clique, if any, that Oldfield belonged to but he was in no hurry to return home for the start of the domestic cricket season after such a dispiriting Ashes series which was somewhat soothed by the news he was listed as one of Wisden Cricketers' Almanack's five Cricketers of the Year. Adding to his growing list of international destinations, Oldfield embarked on a short tour of North America with good mate Johnny Taylor before returning to Sydney in January 1927. Welcomed by reporters, he was queried about a Jack Gregory interview in which he suggested, perhaps facetiously, that Oldfield would be the next Australian captain. "Thank you, no" he replied, explaining that captaincy would be a distraction from his current duties and that he was satisfied being a wicket-keeper .

Oldfield's delayed homecoming saved him from the ignominy of playing in the New South Wales-Victoria Sheffield Shield match in Melbourne over Christmas. In reply to New South Wales's humble 221, a rampant Victorian top order of Woodfull (133), Ponsford (352), Hendry (100) and Ryder (295) helped build the mammoth total of 1107 which remains a First-Class record and with time-limited games is unlikely to be toppled. Arthur Mailey may have wished he had taken a detour as well after returning figures of 4/362 off 64 overs.

THEN CAME BRADMAN

As preparations for the cricket season of 1926-27 were underway in the NSW Southern Highlands, Bowral newspaper the *Southern Mail* of 1 October 1926 alerted cricketers to the arrival of a W.A.Oldfield's Sporting Goods agency in Bong Bong Street opposite the post office. The advertisement promised the country cricketing community an extensive range of equipment with 'all the Best Makes at City Prices'. The franchisee of the store was Bowral's occasional top-order batsman George Bensley whom the previous season was a first-hand witness to the astonishing emergence of a local 17-year-old talent by the name of Donald George Bradman. The short, wiry teenager had re-engaged with the bat and ball after giving the game away in favour of a tennis racquet two years prior. Tales of Bradman's 234 against future teammate Bill O'Reilly's Wingello and 320 not out against Moss Vale in a competition final had reached the Sydney newspapers.

Either through setting-up a Bowral franchise or his regular country promotional tours, it has been part of the Oldfield family history that Bert was possibly the first prominent identity in state cricketing circles to become aware of the Bradman phenomenon.

Oldfield's eldest grandchild Karin Sussmann explains, "because he travelled around New South Wales, he used to supply all the schools with sports equipment, so as part of his rounds he used to watch the local cricket and keep his eyes open for talent. He was in Bowral one time and met Bradman there and said 'come to Sydney'". Karin says that Oldfield also helped Bradman with flannels and equipment when he eventually came to the city to play in trials, "and the rest is history".

If Bert Oldfield had some early influence on Don Bradman's fledgling career, 12 years later at the height of his powers having reached the zenith of Australian cricket, Bradman would have a significant impact on the fate of the legendary wicket-keeper's career at its twilight.

Bradman's break-out 1925-26 club season 1300 runs at an average of over 100, caught the eye of selectors hoping to replenish aging New South Wales playing stocks leading to his selection for the Country Week carnival representing Southern Districts. His performances on the Sydney Cricket Ground numbers 1 and 2 were so impressive that he was already being earmarked for national honours. The *Daily Telegraph* heralded Bradman's batting as, "the essence of freedom and vigor [sic]. He hit the bowling from the start, and used his feet well to anything on the short side. Most of his runs came from powerful shots through the covers and straight drives".

After an initial approach from the Parramatta-based Central Cumberland District Cricket Club, the Bowral lad was lured out of the bush by the Hurstville-based St George club at the tender age of 18. Completely bypassing the apprenticeship of progressing through lower grade cricket, Bradman debuted for the St George firsts on 27 November 1926 against a Petersham line-up including Test player Tommy Andrews and recent Ashes squad tourist Sam

Don Bradman

Everett. Batting at five the new recruit was run out but not before hitting 110 on the picturesque Petersham Oval.

By the time Oldfield turned-out once again for the Gordon 'Kilties' (an allusion to the district's Scottish association) after a 12-month absence, the Australian wicket-keeper was sharing column inches in the newspapers with St George's young batting sensation who had already made it into the New South Wales 2nd XI. On 26 February

1927, the pair met on Hurstville Oval in the St George-Gordon clash but Oldfield would not get to see what the fuss was about with Bradman falling for 11 in the St George victory.

The 33-year-old would have another brush with future batting brilliance in the form of Grenfell Junior's 16-year-old Stanley McCabe. Continuing his regional playing and speaking sojourns, Oldfield joined a Charlie Macartney travelling team with the likes of Tommy Andrews, Arthur Mailey and Jack Ellis to play a combined NSW Central West team at Cowra. While McCabe only made 17 runs in the match, he made up for it with his medium pacers dismissing Oldfield for 46 caught by Bert McCabe – Stan's brother. The cricketing cavalcade continued on to Cootamundra, West Wyalong and Canberra, but his next destination would be the far more exotic climes of Singapore in the winter of 1927.

Due to widening disparity in the quality of cricket between Sydney Grade Cricket and the First-Class level, New South Wales Cricket Association administrators developed what would become a fourth tier of competition in order to bridge the gap. 'Super Grade Cricket' would divide the 16 grade clubs evenly into North, South, East and West zones offering the better club players an elite level to demonstrate their talents with matches played on a Wednesday morning starting at 10am on the Sydney Cricket Ground numbers 1 and 2.

Don Bradman played for South with promising all-rounder and St George teammate Alan Fairfax. East was represented by Waverley veteran Sammy Carter and emerging batsman Jack Fingleton, Arthur Mailey and Warren Bardsley played for West while firebrand leg-spinner Bill O'Reilly was amongst those who turned-out for North.

Oldfield was a notable absence in the North team due to business commitments as were many experienced players who could have boosted the quality of the competition. Held over October and November 1927, Super Grade Cricket was plagued by wash-outs, forfeits and prohibitive scheduling, eventually grinding to an inauspicious halt with the West side ultimately victorious. The concept was never revisited.

※

On the eve of the First-Class season Oldfield's good friend Charlie 'The Governor General' Macartney announced an end to his 22-year career opening a top-order batting position in the New South Wales side. Bradman continued to impress in grade cricket with 125 not out for St George against Sydney University. Overlooked for the first Shield game and a touring New Zealand side, in December Bradman was named in the New South Wales first XI squad to play South Australia in Adelaide on the 16th. Oldfield and Bradman joined their captain Alan Kippax to play a Barrier District team in Broken Hill along the way. Batting at number 7 in his debut match, Bradman played second-fiddle to his captain Kippax who made 143 despite struggling with illness. The debutant looked better against the spinners than the quicks scoring 118 and 33 on an Adelaide Oval wicket more favourable to turn. An 11-wicket haul from Australian leggy Clarrie Grimmett ensured that South Australia narrowly prevailed.

Bradman finished the 1927-28 First-Class season commendably with 416 runs at 46.22 and 2 centuries, but his initial season paled in comparison to the Herculean performances of Victorian

Bill Ponsford's 1217 runs from 6 matches at 152.12 including four centuries with a high score of 437. Despite showing early promise, the youngster received a cold reception from some of his experienced teammates. In an interview with Margaret Geddes in her book *Remembering Bradman*, Victorian spinning all-rounder Doug Ring recalled being approached by Bradman on the deck of the *Orontes* returning home from the 1948 'Invincibles' tour. Bradman opened-up about his early difficulties after moving to Sydney:- "obviously, even then he was showing the signs of greatness and in the New South Wales team there were about six players in the Test team and they all treated him guardedly – they were very suspicious of him. He didn't dislike them but they didn't embrace him either and he found that very hard. I think it coloured his approach to people. He became very guarded", Ring recalled.

The Test players in the New South Wales milieu at the time were Alan Kippax, Tommy Andrews, Arthur Mailey, Jack Gregory, Charlie Kelleway and Bert Oldfield. It can be fairly assumed that Oldfield was part of the 'old guard', some of whom were hardened veterans of the First World War, who enforced a rite of passage on young state cricketers just as they had been tested to make them hardened and prepared to engage.

There was evidently a strict hierarchy in the New South Wales Cricket Team at the time with junior players expected to address their senior colleagues as 'mister _____'. Alan McGilvray recalls in his book *The Game is Not the Same* of interrupting a leadership meeting while reporting to his captain Alan Kippax as the train pulled-out of Sydney's Central Station on the way to Adelaide for a Shield match:

"I gingerly knocked on his compartment door and was bade to enter to find myself in the presence of greats…in earnest discussion with their captain, and the sight of them all together churned my stomach... 'Nice to see you, son,' Kippax offered, with that kindly smile of his. 'Make sure you get an early night'. His words of gentle conversation were iron-clad orders as far as I was concerned. I think I was in bed before the train reached Strathfield in Sydney's western suburbs".

Bert Oldfield appears to have been one of the senior players who concocted initiation pranks to cut eager young players down to size. Once in Adelaide, McGilvray was approached by the veteran keeper with an errand:

"Hey, Al' he beckoned. 'You know you have to go into town and pick up the bats don't you!' Bertie Oldfield, or Mr Oldfield as I then called him according to the upbringing of the day, was something of a national hero...not a man with whom a newcomer to such a Sheffield shield team would argue. 'What bats?' I enquired rather apologetically. He gave me an address. 'Room 15, up the stairs' he said. It's a sports store and they know all about us.' When I got there and dutifully inquired about the bats I was greeted with blank and puzzled looks. 'Bats?' said the girl. 'This is an optician's office.' My red-faced return to my team-mates was greeted with much hilarity. 'Just a bit of fun, son,' Oldfield consoled me. 'Just a bit of fun."

McGilvray didn't get to make his debut on the Adelaide trip, delegated with carrying the drinks as 12th man, but he remained philosophical: "[y]oung players were expected to wear such things. I guess it helped make them tough. It certainly steeled one's determination to succeed; to provide the necessary personal success to win total acceptance into the first class fraternity of the day".

It is not known whether Oldfield was involved, but six years prior to the McGilvray account Don Bradman was sent on his own errand, to Adelaide's seaside suburb of Glenelg in the middle of the night. No doubt he returned empty-handed to the guffaws of his teammates, but there was a precursor episode which revealed a dark side to the New South Wales team. Irving Rosenwater's seminal 1979 biography of Bradman records a sustained ploy which went beyond initiation ritual and bordered on bastardisation. Focussing their attention on the 'new boy', the veterans prodded him with questions to find a chink in the idiosyncratic 19-year-old's armour to exploit:

> 'Meanwhile, they discovered he could play the piano. Was this, they asked him, why his back muscles were in such good shape for cricket? As the train from Sydney proceeded on its long journey, the young Bradman was asked to play on an imaginary keyboard and remove his shirt so that his back muscles could be studied. In the hotel at Adelaide they asked him to do it again, on a real piano – a topless artist of the '20s – while non-cricketing guests were enlisted for the process of 'judging'…Sometimes Bradman laughed, sometimes he did not'.

Unlike McGilvray, Bradman would not view his early experiences as a First-Class cricketer philosophically or as a rite of passage, the ordeal had the opposite effect: making him impenetrable, unknowable and suspicious of his colleagues' motivations.

Bradman was still well down the batting pecking order and was dropped for an Australian XI tour of New Zealand between February and April 1928. Oldfield made his second cricketing trip to Aotearoa with stylish young batsman Archie Jackson chosen ahead of Bradman. Jackson impressed with a tour average of 49.50

and a high score of 198. Oldfield scored a century and averaged 30.16 while taking nine catches and three stumpings.

Upon returning to Australia, Oldfield took a lengthy holiday in the Dubbo region to rest and recuperate over the winter. News of the England squad for the up-coming home Ashes series broke in early-August. Percy Chapman was nominated to lead a side with proven performers Hobbs, Sutcliffe, Tyldesley and Tate while it would introduce some young blood with Surrey batsman Douglas Jardine and fast bowler Harold Larwood, a Nottinghamshire coal miner, who he had played against in tour matches on the 1926 Ashes tour.

Hitting the ground running back in Sydney, Oldfield rode the crest of innovation with the release of the 'Magigraph', a new portable motion picture camera. Sporting performances could be recorded, "then reproduced on a screen providing incalculable benefit for those enthusiasts anxious to succeed. 'Close-ups' and 'slow motion' make it possible to follow every detail", reported the *Referee* of 22 August 1928. A few random, isolated plays captured on newsreel footage in big cricket matches had been around for a few years but lengthy film study of batting, bowling and fielding performances, either to analyse strengths or uncover flaws in player's technique was cutting-edge technology for the time and would have ramifications in the Test arena in the very near future. Demonstrations of the Magigraph were held at Oldfield's Hunter Street store from 6 to 9pm every Friday night.

In November 1928, Oldfield and Bradman played two tour matches for New South Wales and an Australian XI against the Marylebone Cricket Club at the Sydney Cricket Ground. A century in the first game saw Bradman impressing the selectors in favour of his rival Archie Jackson earning him a call-up to the national side.

The first Test of the 1928-29 Ashes series would be the inaugural Test match for the city of Brisbane with the palm-fringed Exhibition Ground chosen to be the venue over the traditional home of Queensland cricket, the Woolloongabba ground. The Australian team selected for Brisbane had all the hallmarks of a side in transition. Captained by Victorian Jack Ryder, fellow long-time all-rounders Stork Hendry, Charlie Kelleway and Jack Gregory made a return to the side as did the experienced Oldfield. Victorians Bill Woodfull and Bill Ponsford and New Zealand-born South Australian Clarrie Grimmett would have the opportunity to

Bert Oldfield using his Magigraph film camera at the Lord's Cricket Ground, London.

build on their early international successes while 31-year-old New South Wales stalwart Alan Kippax returned for just his second Test after debuting in 1925. Don Bradman's fellow debutant was a man more than twice his age in the large form of 46-year-old left-arm finger spinner Bert 'Dainty' Ironmonger.

Batting first, England seemed impossible to dislodge for the ageing Australian seamers. After bowling 41 overs and toiling to take 3 wickets for 142, Jack Gregory's knee cartilage gave-way ending the 33-year-old's cricketing career. Spinners Grimmett and Ironmonger sent down a combined tally of 84 overs to take 3 and 2 wickets respectively before the tourists were finally dismissed for 521 with 'Patsy' Hendren hitting 169. The Australian response was a woeful 122, with only four batsmen reaching double figures, including Bradman with 18. Making matters worse, Charlie Kelleway came down with food poisoning leaving captain Ryder to cobble together a bowling attack consisting of himself, part-time seamer Stork Hendry and the two spinners. Enjoying solid performances again from the middle order, Chapman declared England's innings on 8 for 342, setting Australia an improbable 742 to win. An overnight storm drenching of the 'Ekka' surface conspired with illness and injury to put the depleted Australian Cricket Team to the sword, all-out for 66 on a 'sticky' wicket, a defeat of 675 runs. The only possible highlight for Oldfield would be a clean sheet across both England innings to add to his single catch for the match.

Faced with the loss of a pair of experienced all-rounders in Kelleway and Gregory and with a series already looking like it was falling apart after one match – the Australian selectors tried to plug the gaps. South Australian captain Victor Richardson was brought in to cover Kelleway and open the batting with Woodfull, after Ponsford was sent down the order with a pair of failures in Brisbane. Queensland all-rounder Otto Nothling was picked on unremarkable First-Class form to replace Gregory while Don Bradman was dropped from the side in favour of a third specialist spinner. Bert Ironmonger's record as the oldest Test debutant would only stand for 15 days following the selection of 46 year and 253-day-old St Kilda club teammate, off-spinner Don Blackie.

The Sydney Cricket Ground second Test crowd witnessed another mediocre Australian batting performance with only Woodfull (68), Oldfield (41) and Hendry (37) getting starts in the total of 253. Alan Kippax was perhaps unlucky as he found his bails inexplicably dislodged after a delivery from George Geary which had drifted onto the leg side. In what has gone down in Ashes history as the 'Kippax Incident', bowler's end umpire George Hele called 'over' having not seen anything – along with most of the players and the 20-odd thousand spectators in attendance. An adamant England wicket-keeper George Duckworth appealed and after a few moments of confusion and consternation, square-leg umpire David Elder raised his finger to have Kippax walking to the pavilion, only realising later that he was prohibited from adjudicating the dismissal from that umpiring position.

Bill Ponsford became an additional casualty of the series after sustaining a broken finger off fast bowler Harold Larwood. Chapman's Englishmen ground the Australian bowling attack slowly and mercilessly into the Bulli soil taking 272 overs to amass 636. Walter Hammond enjoyed firm support from his colleagues in his brilliant 251, one of his all-time best innings on his favourite overseas Test ground. The green caps made a better fist of it in the second innings with hundreds to Woodfull and Hendry in a total of 397, but in the end setting England only 16 to win, which they did with 8 wickets in hand.

Despite Charlie Kelleway's recovery from food poisoning and return to the Sheffield Shield, he was no longer in the minds of the selectors and Bradman's 71 not out for New South Wales against Victoria over Christmas was enough to get him a Test recall to replace Ponsford for the third New Years Test in Melbourne. The shuffling of personnel continued with fast-medium Victorian Ernie a'Beckett replacing Nothling and Ironmonger making way for Queensland medium-pacer Ron Oxenham. Another century from Woodfull (107) followed by Kippax (100), Ryder (112) and Bradman (112) could not stop a 3 wicket win to England on the back of a Hammond 200 and the pace and seam attack of Larwood, Tate and Geary. The Ashes were lost to England once again but there was hope for the future with Bradman's maiden century, apart from illness and unavailability, he would be selected for every Australian team for the next two decades. His Melbourne Cricket Ground heroics would soon be eclipsed however, by his New South Wales teammate Archie Jackson in the fourth Test at the Adelaide Oval.

The clean-cut 19-year-old became the seventh debutant in the unfolding disaster that became of the 1928-29 Ashes series

Oldfield keeping behind England's Walter Hammond playing a majestic cover drive during his commanding 1928-29 tour of Australia.

replacing Victor Richardson after his pair of failures opening the batting in the previous Test. Standing at the non-striker's end, Jackson saw his opening partner Woodfull fall for 1, then Stork Hendry (2) and his sports store boss Alan Kippax (3) depart in quick succession in the first innings reply to England's 334. Coming in at 3 for 19, captain Ryder steadied the ship with his young charge who was rising to the occasion with attractive, classical batsmanship. The pair added 126 to the score until the senior partner was adjudged leg-before to slow left-armer Jack White for 63.

At 4 for 179, Bradman joined Jackson at the crease and looked uneasy early, while the Balmain junior accelerated his scoring to reach 97 at lunch on the second day. The new ball was due after the interval with Chapman entrusting the projectile to Harold Larwood's care at the River End. Jackson took strike against the fastest bowler in the world who commenced his long, rhythmic run-up. Larwood pounded the crease hard, releasing an effort ball pitching outside off stump. As if to tenderly caress the ball, the slender Jackson shaped for a cover drive and with perfect timing made contact, the ball ricocheting to the cover-point boundary like a bullet in front of the Member's Pavilion. Jackson's century on debut was met with an explosion of joy and hope from the crowd, Oldfield recalled from his position in the stands, "I distinctly remember how he square drove Larwood to the boundary. It was a risky stroke and one that only a master batsman would even attempt to do that stage of the innings, but it was one typical of Jackson". In a dead-rubber in a lost series, the two young men in the centre of the Adelaide Oval gave the Australian cricketing public hope of better times around the corner.

Jackson's eventual 164 was the highlight in a match where Australia showed stronger fighting instincts, but eventually fell

Archie Jackson

12 short of victory thanks to the turn of Jack White who took 13 wickets for the match. By the final Test in Melbourne, Oldfield and Ryder were the only senior players that had survived to the end of the harrowing ordeal that was the 1928-29 Ashes. Test debutants Tim Wall, Percy Hornibrook and Alan Fairfax donned new Baggy Greens in a consolation victory which saw the locals win by 5 wickets.

In the oppressive tropical heat of Brisbane and blazing sunlight of Sydney, Oldfield had ditched his traditional green cap in favour of a wide-brimmed white floppy hat. Evidently, it appears to be the only Test series in which he replaced his beloved cap for alternative headwear, perhaps feeling that he had jinxed the team in some way. Feeling sorry for Jack Ryder in his final Test as a captain and a player, Oldfield admits that Australia were, "a comparatively weak side-in fact it was somewhat of a patched team. Ryder relied mostly on orthodox methods of captaincy, which did not achieve any outstanding success". He saw positives in the inclusion of Fairfax and Wall and the individual success of Woodfull, Bradman and Jackson but credited the England victory overwhelmingly to Percy Chapman's captaincy abilities.

AN ENDURING PARTNERSHIP

THE AFOREMENTIONED TOUR OF Singapore in the winter of 1927, organised and managed by Oldfield, included his regular travelling companions Macartney and Mailey as well as Test players Warren Bardsley, Edgar Mayne, and Bill Woodfull. After belting a North Australia XI in Darwin along the way, the Australians were victorious in two matches against Singapore in late May and early June. The third match against All-Malaya in Kuala Lumpur ended in a shock defeat for the tourists who were torn apart by British military and expat bowlers. At Seremban, the Oldfield XI atoned for their shock loss with a victory over Southern Malaya in a low-scoring encounter. The fifth match against North Malaya back in Singapore generated widespread enthusiasm but not from the usual British expat or Indian quarters. Oldfield recalled that, "thousands of Malay and Tamil boys thronged the ground, and it is said that never in the history of the country, have the natives and Asiatics [sic] taken such a surprising interest in sport". The tour's final game was a virtual 'scratch match' against an Asiatic XI at Ipoh on 15 June 1927 which included the involvement of Chinese players Ho Ah Loke and

Kwok Ah Keng. Apart from the cricket, the Australians enjoyed activities like elephant rides before returning to Brisbane in July on the *Marella*, the same vessel as the visiting King of Siam.

For the cricket missionary and 33-year-old bachelor, the Singapore tour would have unintended and lifelong consequences after meeting young Sydney woman, Ruth Hunter. Well-known in Sydney social circles, Hunter was the daughter of company director John Hunter and his wife Maud from the eastern Sydney suburb of Randwick. Holidaying in Singapore with her grandmother, Hunter was staying at the Hotel Europe and on one of her walks around the city noticed a game of cricket being played in a park nearby. As a sports enthusiast, she gravitated towards the event and was surprised to find that the match involved a team of Australians – she naturally cheered for her compatriots. The participants all dispersed following the game and she returned to the hotel continuing her travel itinerary for another few days. Returning to Australia on the *Marella*, Hunter was surprised when hearing the news that the Australian cricketers she had watched were also on board.

The first day out of Java, Oldfield and Hunter were formally introduced and in the evening while she was enjoying the sunset on deck he struck-up a conversation and took a stroll with her in the fading light. The pair was frequently in each other's company on the way back to Australia, overseen by Hunter's chaperone, but parted upon returning with no firm plans to stay in contact. After a few chance re-acquaintances in the following weeks, Oldfield invited Hunter out for afternoon tea which led to dinners, parties and games of golf and tennis together.

After a year-long courtship, Oldfield approached John Hunter and asked for his daughter's hand in marriage, the engagement sealed with a single-stone platinum diamond ring. The engagement party was celebrated in the ballroom of the Ambassadors club in Sydney on 23 September 1928 which was also Ruth's 21st birthday. The party was attended by Arthur Mailey, Johnny Taylor, Oldfield's friend Edgar Rofe who opened the batting for the Petersham club, sisters Linda Oldfield and Lyle Saddler with her husband Tony.

In an interview with the *Daily Telegraph* of 26 September 1928, Hunter revealed that she was an all-round sportsperson, participating in dancing, swimming, ice-skating, golf and tennis. She divulged that she was also helping her fiancée train by throwing balls at him, saying "I never got a ball past him". Of Oldfield she said, "Bert and I have had some great rounds of golf… but he isn't very keen on skating. Still there is really nothing one can take up that the other cannot join in".

In February, bowls of red roses decorated the tables at a gift tea for Hunter held at the Oceanic Hotel in Coogee and attended by Oldfield's sisters Beatrice and Maud. On the Wednesday night before the wedding, Oldfield was the guest of honour at a bachelor's dinner held at the Civic Club in Sydney, complete with miniature cricket bats personalised with the guest's names and menus printed on the other side.

On the evening of Saturday, 23 March 1929 the couple was married at St Jude's Anglican Church in Randwick, with the service officiated by Reverend Canon W. J. Cakebread. Such was the public interest in the nuptials that six policemen were on duty to control a crowd estimated at around 2000. The *Truth* newspaper described the bride as "simply lovely" in her dress of "dull ivory white satin, draped at the side to form an uneven hemline" with a veil of, "gorgeous Brussels lace over pink tulle, the whole thing forming a train…held in place with a coronet of pearls, rhinestones, and orange blossom". Her bridesmaids were her sisters Jean and Risse and friends Irene Mayo and Lurline Toohey. Oldfield's best man was teammate Johnny Taylor with friends Bob Herring, Jack Martin and Edgar Rofe as groomsmen. Charlie Macartney and Arthur Mailey also attended the service.

The wedding reception, back at the Ambassador's ballroom, was cricket-themed with the bridal table adorned with a green and gold flower arrangement of stumps, bat and ball. The newlyweds received gifts from many in the cricketing fraternity including glass brandy goblets from England captain Percy Chapman.

In typical Oldfield tradition, the couple boarded the *Orford* for their honeymoon to England via Ceylon (current day Sri Lanka) and the Continent which would be a mix of business and pleasure before returning home to live with the Hunter family at 'Casbah' on Dudley Street, Randwick.

The couple welcomed daughter Ruth Mary into the world on 7 January 1930 and in March 1932 another daughter, Judith Ann was born. In 1931, the young family moved into a home of their own, the impressive 'Poitiers' located at 66 Springdale Road,

The Oldfield home at 'Poitiers' 66 Springdale Road, Killara.

Killara. Built in 1904 on a large block, the spacious five bedroom brick residence was ornamented with large arched windows and entranceway, high plaster ceilings, timber joinery and broad fireplaces. In March 2017, the property sold for $5.45 million with much of the home still in its original state.

Of married life at Poitiers, Oldfield's eldest grand-daughter Karin Sussmann said her grandmother Ruth settled into the role of being the wife of a prominent sportsman. "She was just what he needed, because he would rock-up to the house with a whole team – because there wasn't a phone [to warn her] – and she would have to find food in the pantry to feed them and she was able to manage it well. She never let him down. After he retired from playing [Bert] would take teams overseas to Hong Kong, Ethiopia and South Africa and she would always go with him and support him. She was always supportive".

A GREAT DEPRESSION

Whilst honeymooning in England and likely reflecting on the long and disastrous series he had just endured, Oldfield reportedly admitted to an *Evening News* journalist in May 1929 that he was considering retirement from First-Class cricket, quoted as saying, "I feel I've had enough". The account included that the allegedly-jaded wicket-keeper had revealed that he had declined a bet from a friend that he would be a lock-in for the 1930 Ashes tour of England.

Reporting Oldfield's concerning revelation, the Sydney *Referee* heaped praise on him as a cricketer and businessman, revealing that, "war effects may still show in him, as they do in most men who saw active service in the Great War...His fighting spirit is implacable. He may have dropped a little below his best form behind the wickets in the latest Test matches, but where is the man who has not had moments when he has been a trifle 'off colour'?".

By mid-July, Oldfield made known that he was still keen on playing top-line cricket and that some of what was previously reported had been exaggerated. About to embark from Liverpool for the couple's return home, when asked about the up-coming 1930 Ashes, Oldfield was reported in syndicated papers on 22

July 1929 as saying, "I think England has much talent but believe Australia will come out on top in the next Test series. She is rich with cricket possibilities and should meet with great success". Settling into married life back home he continued to assure the press that he was willing to keep playing provided he had the confidence of the New South Wales and Australian selectors.

Constantly in search of innovative marketing strategies and campaigns for his business, and seemingly ahead of his time, Oldfield projected a 'Magigraph' instructional film of himself wicket-keeping, business partner Macartney batting and Arthur Mailey bowling in the window of his Hunter Street store. The boom times and prosperity of the 'Roaring '20s' that he had enjoyed in growing his business was about to come to an abrupt end with the crash of the New York Stock Exchange across September and October 1929. Like the war many years earlier, the effects of the economic collapse on the other side of the world would send shockwaves around the globe resulting in unemployment and poverty, reducing disposable incomes and discretionary spending on non-essential items…like sporting equipment.

In spite of the gathering economic storm, Sydney Grade Cricket commenced for the 1929-30 season with youngsters Bradman and Jackson hitting 180 not out for St George and 115 for Balmain in the first round respectively. Oldfield returned for the Gordon club which now enjoyed the services of his best man Johnny Taylor, along with ageing former internationals Kelleway and Macartney, the 'Kilties' had a formidable batting order that season with the latter knocking 112 at the age of 43.

Without Test matches scheduled during the summer, the 1929-30 Sheffield Shield competition was devoted to building a side capable of regaining the Ashes in 1930. Charlie Kelleway and Tommy Andrews became victims of the state selector's youth policy and would no longer be considered for First-Class honours. As one of a dwindling band of senior players, Oldfield's first experience of state captaincy resulted in a victory for the baby Blues against Queensland in Brisbane on 12 November 1929. Another youngster now under his wing to join the likes of Bradman and Jackson was Grenfell's Stan McCabe who had dismissed him at the match in Cowra three years prior, now debuting at the age of 19.

On 22 November 1929, New South Wales faced a non-Test Marylebone Cricket Club touring team including Duleepsinhji, Arthur Gilligan and Frank Woolley at the Sydney Cricket Ground. Chasing a wide-ball, Oldfield broke the index finger on his left hand in two places resulting in him missing the rest of the match while batsman and part-time keeper Arthur Allsopp wore the gloves. With a doctor's recommendation that he not risk further injury to his fractured digit, Oldfield notified the New South Wales Cricket Association of his unavailability for selection. Victorian keeper Jack Ellis took Oldfield's place in a December Test trial while Waverley's Hugh Davidson and Hammy Love, back from playing for Victoria, shared Oldfield's position in the New South Wales team for the remainder of the 1929-30 season.

The future Australian Test side started taking shape with incredible performances particularly from the batsmen. Bradman had hit a world record First-Class score of 452 not out against Queensland at the S.C.G. and was carried off the field by his opponents in acknowledgement of the feat. By the end of the season he had scored 1586 runs at an average of 113.28. In spite of injury and illness to all, Woodfull, Jackson, Kippax and McCabe

Bradman chaired off the S.C.G. by his Queensland opponents after scoring a world record 452 not out.

pushed their claims with averages exceeding 50 runs-an-innings. Of the bowlers, Clarrie Grimmett topped the wicket aggregates with 82 at 23.69 while Queensland bowling pair Alec Hurwood and Percy Hornibrook and New South Wales all-rounder Alan Fairfax also looked promising with the ball.

While still being top-pick by the pundits for the 1930 Ashes tour of England, Oldfield's 6 catches and 3 stumpings from only three matches and having to rest his hand until February was a serious cause for concern. No doubt soothing the pain of injury and uncertainty about his playing future was the birth of daughter Ruth Mary on 7 January. For a travelling businessman and semi-professional cricketer, the time at home with wife Ruth and the baby would most certainly have been cherished by the first-time father.

In February, the national selectors took a gamble on Oldfield's untested finger by naming him in the Ashes squad with South Australian keeper Charlie Walker as his back-up. The team included Ponsford, Bradman, Jackson, Kippax, McCabe, a'Beckett, Fairfax, Grimmett, Wall, Hornibrook and Hurwood with Woodfull named as captain and Richardson vice-captain. Former Test cricketer and team physician Dr Roy Minnett cleared Oldfield's finger as having healed sufficiently and forwarded his report to the Board of Control. As a precaution, he played only as a batsman for Gordon against Paddington at Hampden Park in his last match in Australia before leaving for England.

In a gesture to foster the game in the smaller states, the Australian Cricket Team played Tasmania and West Australia on home soil *en route* to England in March 1930. Oldfield was again 'in the wars' in his first game back as wicket-keeper in the initial match at Launceston, keeping up to the stumps to fast-medium bowler Alan Fairfax. Seventeen-year-old Tasmanian Jack Badcock, who would later play Test cricket after moving to South Australia, faced a beamer from the lanky all-rounder. Oldfield expected that Badcock would step inside the line and hook the ball to the square-leg boundary, but at the last minute he ducked – the ball striking the keeper flush on the forehead. Vice-captain Victor Richardson replaced Oldfield who had left the field to get treatment. Fairfax confided to Richardson that he had deliberately bowled what he termed his 'Boo-Ball' in an attempt to spook the batsman and admitted to the substitute keeper that he was surprised Oldfield was not expecting the delivery. In the interest of self-preservation Richardson, who had also played baseball for Australia, hastily devised a pitcher-catcher style signal with Fairfax to warn him of the particular ball. Charlie Walker deputised for Oldfield in the remaining Tasmania game in Hobart and the Western Australia match in Perth before the month-long voyage to England.

The Australians arrived in London to be met by the traditional inclement weather to hamper early training sessions. Players participated in Anzac Day 1930 wreath-laying ceremonies and paid their respects at war cemeteries around London. Attending an Anzac reunion at Australia House, former Corporal Oldfield conversed with retired General Sir Ian Hamilton who commanded the ill-fated Gallipoli campaign in 1915.

In the early tour matches, second-time tourist Bill Woodfull was impressive with the bat and Grimmett was outstanding with the ball, including 10 for 39 against a star-studded Yorkshire – but the most striking thing was Don Bradman's quick adjustment to English conditions. Characteristically still as the bowler approached, his eye seemed to pick-up the ball very early, his quick feet positioning him to make perfectly-timed drives and pull shots invariably along the ground, into gaps and to the boundary. Leading up to the first Test, the 21-year-old had scored 236 against Worcestershire, 185 not out versus Leicestershire and 252 against Surrey.

In the first Test at the Trent Bridge ground in Nottingham, a shared effort from the Australian bowling attack saw England bowled out for 270. In what may have felt like a repeat of the previous series, Australia collapsed to 144 with Alan Kippax fighting a lone hand with 64 not out. With England having set Australia 428 runs to win in their second innings, Bradman sought to redeem his failure of 8 in the first innings. Oldfield recalled that Bradman, "on whom our hopes now rested, continued to defy the attack with the skill and determination of a veteran. It was certainly a magnificent exhibition of courage, patience, and defence, a quality which hitherto had not been associated with his name". Despite his 131, Bradman's efforts were in vain as Australia lost the Test by 93 runs.

England again batted first in the second Test at Lord's with debutant Duleepsinhji scoring 173 in the total of 425. The Australian batting order more than redeemed itself by punishing an attack led by George 'Gubby' Allen, Maurice Tate and Jack White with 6 declared for 729. Watched by King George V in the Lord's Pavilion, Bradman (254) and Woodfull (155) topped the score with Ponsford (81) and Kippax (83) in support. Thanks to 6 for 167 by in-form Clarrie Grimmett, England was dismissed for 375 setting 72 for victory. Australia reached the total with 7 wickets in hand to level the series.

Batting first in the third Test at Headingley in Leeds, Bradman at number three arrived early to the crease with dismissal of Archie Jackson for 1. Demonstrating his characteristic footwork and aggressive stroke-play he belted the England attack to all parts of the ground ominously reaching his century before lunch. Batting partners Woodfull (50) and Kippax (77) took a backseat to Bradman's explosive innings which he took to a record-breaking 309 not out at stumps on the first day. Caught-behind by George Duckworth off Maurice Tate the next day for 334, he had made the highest score in Test cricket history in 448 balls with 46 boundaries in Australia's innings of 566. Walter Hammond scored 113 in England's reply of 391 but rain thwarted an Australian victory with England's second innings stranded on 3 for 95 and the game ending in a draw. Charlie Walker stood-in for Oldfield in matches against Scotland between the Tests in mid-July 1930. The old combatants only managed to play an innings each in the rain-affected fourth test at Old Trafford in Manchester, before it was officially drawn.

A gift given by an admirer in good faith to Don Bradman in recognition for his world record Test score of 334 would have an unintended consequence of isolating him even further from his teammates. Anglo-Australian soap manufacturer Arthur Whitelaw was so impressed by the innings that he gifted Bradman with the princely sum of £1000 – around $150,000 today. Syndicated newspapers on 14 July 1930 reported Whitlaw as saying, "I thought Bradman's performance merited such recognition as it would be useful to a young fellow on the threshold of his career. Boxers get much more for far less important achievements. We must encourage our cricketers in every way possible since cricket is the greatest of all games. This is not so much a gift as a mark of appreciation on behalf of Australians". The rest of the Australian Cricket Team did not go unacknowledged by Whitelaw's generosity – each presented with an ashtray. In his 1996 biography *Bradman*, Charles Williams revealed that the contrast in the gifts did not go unnoticed by Bradman's teammates, "the occasion was turned by some into sourness, particularly when they asked him to celebrate the gift by entertaining them to dinner – a suggestion which Bradman coolly declined to take up".

The thousand yard stare: veteran Oldfield on the England tour in 1930.

A Great Depression

With the 1930 Ashes series locked at one-all, Australia had to win the final Test at the Oval in south London to prevent England retaining the Urn that they had held since 1926. England started affirmatively with Herbert Sutcliffe scoring 161 in the first innings total of 405. The Australian batting order carefully constructed a formidable innings in response. The Victorian opening firm of Woodfull and Ponsford built a 159-run partnership with the former stonewalling and the latter the aggressor until Ponsford was bowled by Ian Peebles for 110. Bradman now at the crease, the dogged Woodfull was dismissed soon after for 54 off 196 balls, the score 2 for 190. Kippax contributed 28 to the total until he was dismissed with the score on 3 for 263, bringing Archie Jackson to the centre. Jackson was not his usual stylish, expressive self and took on the duty of partnership anchor while Bradman attacked the bowling at the other end, but with increasing caution.

Patchy rain over London had led to multiple delays resulting in the teams going on and off the field at frustrating intervals. The uncovered pitch was now wet and unpredictable. With the welfare of his players always paramount, captain Woodfull had petitioned the umpires to delay a restart late on Day 3, but the officials were convinced by England leader Bob Wyatt's appeals to resume. Tired, frustrated and wicket-less, fast bowler Harold Larwood was gifted with a last-minute crack at the young Australians. The deliveries from the express paceman spat steeply off a length repeatedly hitting Bradman and Jackson until stumps with overnight rain ensuring the conditions would continue for Day 4. The next day Jackson's left side was a mass of bruises, including a blow to his jaw. While on 175, Bradman was hit in the chest by Larwood which doubled him over in pain. The ordeal left the youthful pair looking somewhat beyond their years, photographs taken as the pair walked onto the field from

101

a break in play captured drawn and jaded facial expressions like the game they were playing was no longer fun.

Keen observers on the ground and in the stands for the first time noticed a change in Bradman's confident demeanour and a new hesitation in his batting as he weaved and flinched at the red projectile which he had so confidently dispatched to every corner of the ground. Also trained on his every movement in the stands at The Oval was a film camera which would provide invaluable tactical analysis for future England captain, Douglas Jardine.

Any glint of hope for retaining the Ashes was fading for the Englishmen with the Australians passing their first innings total after the loss of only three wickets as Bradman and Jackson continued weathering the storm. With the score on 506, Jackson became the fourth wicket to fall, taking 311 balls to accumulate his innings of 73 in a partnership of 246. Bradman was the next to be dismissed, caught-behind by Duckworth for Larwood's only wicket in the innings, for 232 off 417 balls. McCabe (54), Fairfax (53) and Oldfield (34) continued to compound England's woes with the tally finishing on 695 runs. Australia's rookie left-arm orthodox spinner Percy Hornibrook became the unlikely hero taking career-best figures of 7 for 92 to humble the England middle-order. The home side's 251 fell short by an innings and 39 runs which handed the Ashes back to Australia with a 2-1 series victory.

Oldfield's performance during the series was solid but not outstanding. He took 13 catches and 3 stumpings but allowed 65 runs in byes past him – a hazard of keeping up to stumps to both seamers and spinners. His batting also took a hit during the series with returns of 96 runs at an average of 16 with a high score of 43. What he got to watch from the pavilion and on the field during the 17th Australian touring team to England in 1930 however, was truly astonishing. He had started playing cricket during the last reverberations of the game's Golden Age where memories of Victor Trumper still lingered. He had played against the world's greatest in Jack Hobbs and in the twilight of that legend's career the phenomenon that was Donald Bradman would emerge to mesmerize the cricketing world. Of the world's new batting sensation, Oldfield said, "I cannot speak too highly of Don Bradman's individual performances. We were actually witnessing them. It will be far more difficult to judge the magnitude of his deeds when we read about them years hence".

As the 1930 Ashes tourists returned home in early November, the press was rife with the usual rumours regarding the nation's elite cricketers. It was credibly assumed that Bradman would be the subject of lucrative approaches from Lancashire League clubs while speculation mounted that Oldfield was headed for retirement. Back in Sydney, the New South Wales players attended a formal reception to welcome them home with each being modest about their own achievements and heaping praise on their teammate's performances.

Oldfield told the *Sydney Morning Herald* of 7 November 1930, "[i]t was definitely the most enjoyable tour I have yet had…Realise, we were meeting with success the whole way through and yet had to fight for it. Contrast that with 1921 when we were infinitely more superior. This last tour was far more pleasing…We had a happy tour. Yet all the time we were conscious of the economic conditions in our own country. I think that inspired us on the field. It seemed to prepare us for a sense of duty". There was no doubt from the enthusiastic welcome home what the Ashes victory meant for Australians caught in the grip of the Great Depression, but on a personal level the priority would be reintegrating into family life after eight months away and reacquainting himself with his 11-month-old daughter Ruth Mary who had grown and changed so much.

CALM BEFORE THE STORM

THE AUSTRALIAN CRICKET TEAM had not long recovered their land-legs before the inaugural Test series against the West Indies over the summer of 1930-31. Granted status in the most elite level of the sport by the 1926 Imperial Cricket Conference, the burgundy-capped multi-jurisdiction team from the Caribbean brought with them fast bowling, athletic fielding and an invigorating presence to the cricket scene.

Fortuitously, a tour match between New South Wales and the West Indies at the Sydney Cricket Ground gave Oldfield precious time at home before the travelling resumed. The nifty keeper was in his element as the tourists were frequently lured out of their creases on the turning Bulli soil deck. Oldfield took five stumpings and four catches in the match and was stumped himself for 21 by his opposite number, Ivan Barrow. New South Wales winning the match by 4 wickets.

The Adelaide Oval became another happy hunting ground for stumping opportunities in the first Test with Oldfield taking three pegs off Clarrie Grimmett and one off Alec Hurwood. The West Indians scored 296 in the first innings with contributions from Edward Bartlett (84) Clifford Roach (56) and captain George

Grant (52). Facing the West Indian trio of George Francis (2 for 43), Learie Constantine (1 for 89) and Herman Griffith (2 for 69) for the first time the Australians replied with 376, Alan Kippax (146) and Stan McCabe (90) the stand-outs. Grimmett took his tally to 11 wickets for the match as the tourists were bowled out for 249 in their second innings. Bill Ponsford (92) and Archie Jackson (70) chased the 172 required runs without loss, opening the series at 1-0.

Played under blazing sunlight on New Year's Day 1931, the second Test at the Sydney Cricket Ground commenced with an onslaught from Bill Ponsford. Playing a virtual lone-hand, the Victorian opener hit 183 assisted mainly by Woodfull (58) batting at number 6 in support with the first innings total finishing on 369. The West Indies would again succumb to the turn of the Sydney pitch, dismissed for 107 and 90 with spinners Grimmett, Hurwood and Ironmonger sharing most of the victims.

Bradman awoke from his two-Test slumber with 223 and partook in a 229-run partnership for the second wicket with Ponsford (109) in the third Test at the Brisbane Exhibition Ground. Australia's total of 558 was too much for the West Indies replies of 193 and 148. The brilliant George Headley offered the only defiance against the Australian spinners with 102 not out in the first innings.

It took Australia only two days to defeat the West Indies in the fourth Test at the Melbourne Cricket Ground. In their first innings, the Windies were bowled-out for 99 courtesy of 'Dainty' Ironmonger's 7 for 23. Captain Woodfull declared Australia's reply on 8 for 328 which included another Bradman century (152). Ironmonger increased his wicket tally to 11 for the match as the Caribbean side were dismissed for 107.

Youngster Archie Jackson had not been his usual chipper self and his performances progressively declined in the series to the point he was dropped for the final Test in Sydney in favour of Victorian Keith Rigg. The unbeaten Australians experienced a change in fortune however, with the team's vulnerability to express pace and rain-affected wickets coming back to haunt them. Centuries from left-handed opener Frank Martin (123) and George Headley (105) took the West Indies to 6 for 350 when captain Grant made a surprise declaration. The pace trio of Francis, Constantine and Griffith with the addition of Martin's slow left-armers stifled the Australians to have them bowled out for 224. Another daring declaration at 5 for 124 saw the West Indies set the home side 250 to win only to have them dismissed 30 runs short. The lone Australian batsman to exceed 50 runs was all-rounder Alan Fairfax which he did twice, top-scoring in both innings (54 and 60 not out) – Australia winning the series 4-1.

Oldfield looked back on the series, with great affection for the West Indies players saying, "[a]n entertaining lot they were, too, cricketers prepared to mix big hitting with stone-walling…a combination of interesting personalities. Individually they were a keen band of cricketers, fine sportsmen, with outstanding stars in Headley and Constantine. From an educational point of view the tour was eminently successful to our visitors in the development of their players".

With Australian, New South Wales and Gordon commitments completed for another season, Oldfield would not be hanging-up the flannels and storing the keeping gloves and pads just yet. The Union Theatres distribution group decided to capitalise on the success and popularity of the reinvigorated Australian Cricket Team by making a film of their exploits. *'That's Cricket'* was directed by 30-year-old Ken G. Hall who had written and directed war film *'The Exploits of the Emden'* in 1928 and would go on to direct Australian classics like *'On Our Selection'* and *'Dad and Dave'*. Produced at Cinesound City in Bondi and filmed mainly on the Sydney Cricket Ground number 2, Oldfield, Woodfull, Bradman, Ponsford, McCabe, Grimmett and Kippax demonstrated their respective disciplines for the cameras with elevated shots, slow-motion capture and recorded sound. With a school master's formality, captain Bill Woodfull introduced the film explaining that through, "the means of the talking screen with its amazing power to so lucidly demonstrate and explain most things we can do something to foster cricket in this our native land". Each player was introduced for the cameras with a short biographical detail, Woodfull joking in Bradman's case that he had "more records than a gramophone company". Bradman responded to Woodfull's quip in a monologue at the conclusion of the film explaining that his teammates all share credit in any records that he had made. *'That's Cricket'* premiered and was screened across the country from April 1931 with audiences treated to slow-motion close-ups of Kippax's elegant late-cut, Woodfull advancing out of his crease to hit a cover-drive and Oldfield's dexterity behind the stumps.

Not only would the cricket fans of rural New South Wales get to watch the Australian wicket-keeper in action on the big screen but they also got to see the man in person on a follow-up speaking tour. Over the winter of 1931, Oldfield spoke at schools and club events while promoting his business in towns including Inverell, Maitland, Gilgandra, Parkes, Forbes and Dubbo.

In the summer of 1931-32, the South African Cricket Team was scheduled to resume Test cricket with Australia after a decade hiatus and return for their first tour of Australia in over 20 years. The Springbok's wicket-keeping captain Jock Cameron would be bringing over a youthful team including his back-up keeper Edward van der Merwe who was given pointers as a school boy by Bert Oldfield himself at one of his school visits on the 1921 tour.

Queensland hosted New South Wales for the first Sheffield

Shield game of the season at the Woolloongabba ground in Brisbane on November 6 1931. Having won the toss, Queensland captain Frank Gough advised offsider Alan Kippax that the home team would bat first. Shortly before taking the field, Oldfield and the rest of the New South Wales team were plunged into a state of shock after finding their teammate Archie Jackson coughing-up blood in the dressing room. Jackson had been getting over what was believed to be a bout of influenza from the previous week and was admitted to a Brisbane hospital for the duration of the match – 12th man Jack Fingleton his last minute replacement.

In their first innings, Queensland struggled against the seam attack of Fairfax, McCabe and Gordon Amos to be dismissed for 109 on a lively Gabba wicket spiced-up by a touch of rain. The second over of the New South Wales reply, bowled by Aboriginal fast bowler Eddie Gilbert, would go down in Australian cricketing folklore. Opening batsman Wendell Bill had watched his partner Jack Fingleton face the first over off Hugh Thurlow conclude in a maiden – now it was his turn. The short, wiry Gilbert sprang-in to the crease on his innocuous short run and unleashed a thunderbolt which pounced spitefully off the deck. A startled Bill, half-ducking and half-fending at the ball in an attempt to protect himself, resulted in the ball clipping his gloves and lobbing into the welcoming grasp of Len Waterman a pitch-length behind.

Number three batsman Don Bradman arrived at the crease but he was facing a vastly different Queensland attack to the one he slaughtered on the Sydney Cricket Ground two years prior. Gilbert worked Bradman over with what the latter claimed to be the fastest bowling he had ever faced. The first delivery he got well behind, blocking it safely.

The next three balls saw Bradman ducking a bouncer, ending on his back to evade a rising ball and with the bat knocked out of his hands by the force of the delivery after attempting a hook shot – the fastest ball Bradman said he ever faced. On the sixth ball Gilbert pitched another delivery short of a length, Bradman reacting too late to play a pull shot clipped the ball on its way into Waterman's waiting gloves. Gilbert raised his arms skyward in jubilation as the batsman swung around disorientated. Bradman 0 – New South Wales 2 for 0.

Alan Kippax survived the last two deliveries of Gilbert's 8-ball over, but having reached 16 was struck on the head trying to hook a bouncer from 'Pud' Thurlow and was rushed to the Mater Misericordiae Hospital for treatment – the same infirmary as Archie Jackson who would be admitted there for the entire week.

As the pitch flattened-out, the New South Wales batsmen stabilised the innings with Fingleton (93), Oldfield (46) and McCabe (229 not out) contributing to the total of 432. In spite of the glorious fleeting moment of dominance, the maroons collapsed in their second innings with 85, handing the royal blues a victory by an innings and 238 runs but concerns about Jackson's health issues and Kippax and Bradman's vulnerability to the fast, short ball lingered.

Oldfield was back at the Gabba, this time in the Baggy Green for the first Test against South Africa. In Australia's opening account, Oldfield (56 not out) took over from Bradman (226) as the mainstay of the innings partnering with the lower order to get the score to 450. South Australian quick Tim Wall (2 for 39 and 5 for 14) and Victorian slow left-armer Bert Ironmonger (5 for 42 and 4 for 44) helped demolish the Springboks (170 and 117) to give Australia an innings and 163 run victory.

Clarrie Grimmett (4 for 28 and 4 for 44) dominated the South African batting with his lobbed wrist spin in the second Test at the Sydney Cricket Ground. A pair of centuries from Bradman

(112) and Rigg (127) in Australia's only innings of 469 saw the tourists defeated once again by an innings and 155.

In the third Test in Melbourne, Oldfield suffered the humiliation of his first 'pair' in Test cricket but atoned for it with every wicket-keeper's ambition – stumping the opposition keeper, Jock Cameron. The beleaguered South Africa were more competitive in the New Year's Test with a century from Ken Viljoen (111) but centuries from Woodfull (161) and Bradman (167) and 7 wickets from Ironmonger resulted in a 169-run win for Australia.

Grimmett (7 for 116 and 7 for 83) was devastating again, this time on his home ground at the Adelaide Oval in the fourth Test. An unlucky Bradman was stranded on 299 not out when his batting partner Pud Thurlow was run out for a duck in Australia's second innings of 513. In their second innings, the Springboks could only manage to set Australia 73 for victory which they did without loss.

The fifth Test at the Melbourne Cricket Ground would mark the completion of South Africa's utter humiliation on Australian soil. After winning the toss and batting, Victorian pairing Laurie Nash (4 for 18) and Bert Ironmonger (5 for 6) tore-up the South African batting order, bowling them out for 36 in an-hour-and-a-half. With the wicket still difficult to bat on, Australia reached 153 with contributions from Fingleton (40) and Kippax (42). After a washed-out Day 2, South Africa were put to the sword on the third by Ironmonger (6 for 18) and Bill O'Reilly (3 for 19) – dismissed for 45. Owing largely to the Second World War, Australia and South Africa would not contest another Test series for 17 years until Australia toured in 1949-50.

Back in Sydney, fresh from the Test series, Bert and Ruth Oldfield welcomed another daughter, Judith Ann, into the family in March 1932. While confessing to the *Daily Telegraph* of 15 March that he was hoping for a boy, a proud Oldfield said, "[Judith] has dark curly hair like the first baby, Ruth Mary, and she weighs the same- 7 1/2lb". In reference to an up-coming Shield game in which Oldfield was scheduled to captain, the *Daily Telegraph* writer appealed that, "if he should fumble the ball or miss a catch behind on Saturday barrackers should let him off lightly". In the match on the 19th, Oldfield took two catches but leaked 13 byes in the loss to South Australia at the Sydney Cricket Ground but it did not impact New South Wales winning the trophy once again.

In the Gordon versus St George mid-April clash at Chatswood Oval, Oldfield had the unfortunate vantage point in watching Don Bradman demolish an ageing Gordon attack including Kelleway and Macartney. Bradman hit 201 in two hours and 51 minutes with 27 fours and two sixes but eventually fell to an Oldfield stumping. On 30 April 1932, Bradman married his childhood sweetheart Jessie Menzies at St Paul's Anglican Church in Burwood and like the Oldfield's three years before, required police to deal with the intense public interest. The newlywed Bradmans embarked on a cricketing honeymoon to the United States and Canada over the northern summer with an Arthur Mailey touring team. Oldfield would normally have been a guaranteed member of the tour which would have seen him brush shoulders with Hollywood luminaries Boris Karloff, Aubrey Smith, Myrna Loy and baseball legend 'Babe' Ruth, but family and business interests took priority. Fifty-four year-old Sammy Carter performed wicket-keeping duties for the tour in the twilight of his playing career but disaster would befall him when permanently losing sight in one eye after being struck by the ball keeping up to the stumps.

FAST LEG THEORIES

Possibly through exhaustion or a reoccurrence of his war trauma, Oldfield was admitted to a private hospital for an undisclosed 'breakdown in health' requiring complete rest for a fortnight in July 1932. After discharge, the 37-year-old again chose to convalesce in the country with an aim to resuming grade cricket in October. Oldfield's friend and business partner Charlie Macartney expressed concerns in the Sydney *Sportsman* of 1 October 1932 about the possible "mental exhaustion" of players like Bradman, Kippax and McCabe who had just returned from Mailey's strenuous tour of North America in the lead-up to the Ashes. Of his old mate, he confided, "Bertie Oldfield has returned to business, looking in the pink of condition, and any doubts as to his appearing in the important fixtures of this season can now be set at rest". He also confirmed that Oldfield would be missing the first two rounds for Gordon while he continued to recharge.

Oldfield's return to cricket was in a New South Wales selection trial match where he captained his eponymous team against the Kippax XI on October 16. Test cricketer and *The Sun* journalist Jack Fingleton reported from the Sydney Cricket Ground number 2 that Oldfield, "missed Kippax off a difficult catch in [the] first over, but after that settled down and kept magnificently. His catch of Kippax on the leg-side was a gem, but right through he gathered cleanly on the leg and from the field, and when two of Kippax's batsmen walked up the pitch and missed the ball, Oldfield did the rest with precision and certainty. He was in rare form". The recent rest and recuperation seemed to agree with Oldfield's batting also as he took the long-handle to the Kippax XI's slow bowlers in his innings of 24, Fingleton describing the following: "[o]ne six by Oldfield was a beauty, and spectators had time to ponder whether it would go out of the ground altogether, or land on the back of several horses grazing quietly on the hill. It did neither, but that hit scared a ground attendant".

On the main ground Don Bradman captained his own XI against a team led by Hammy Love. Bradman scored a typically dominant innings of 145 along with 19-year-old Marrickville batsman Bill Brown making a promising early appearance with 73 runs. The Kippax and Bradman XIs would win the day, but soon after whether Bradman would play in the 1932-33 Ashes series at all would be under a cloud. Anxious about his financial and professional situation, and after intense interest and lucrative offers to go to England and play cricket professionally, Bradman signed a three-way contract designed to keep him in Australia. Sydney radio station 2UE, Associated Newspapers and sporting goods retailer F.J. Palmer and Sons retained Bradman's services to write, broadcast and promote for the companies under a two-year contract. The Australian Board of Control for Cricket declared however, that Bradman would be ineligible for Test selection as only cricketers where journalism was their sole source of income like Jack Fingleton, could write about the game. This would not be the case for Bradman due to the other aspects of the contract, but Bradman stood firm saying he would abide by his agreement. Ultimately, Associated Newspapers relented and released Bradman from his writing obligations and he was available for Test selection once more.

Soon after the New South Wales selection trial, Bradman, Fingleton and Stan McCabe boarded a train for the long transcontinental journey to Perth to play in a combined team against the newly-landed English tourists. The touring side included batsmen Herbert Sutcliffe, Wally Hammond, Bob Wyatt, the Nawab of Pataudi, Maurice Leyland, wicket-keepers George Duckworth and Leslie Ames, fast bowling all-rounder Gubby Allen, left-arm orthodox spinner Hedley Verity and fast bowlers Harold Larwood, Bill Voce and Bill Bowes. Captaining the team was the Surrey amateur Douglas Jardine, a Winchester College old boy and University of Cambridge graduate, who had a reputation for being dour and aloof and harbouring an intense dislike of Australians.

Jardine's close friend and Surrey County Cricket Club captain Percy Fender made way for him to lead the county team in March 1932 which in-turn paved the way for him to become England captain. The 'Bradman problem' would be the key challenge to confront any leader of a team chosen to mount a campaign against Australia. Jardine was not present at his county ground, The Oval in 1930 to witness Bradman's difficulty against Larwood's pace on a wet wicket but cricketing circles were rife with accounts and theories.

In late July, the Nottinghamshire county team travelled down to London to play Surrey at home and brought with them the pace pairing of Larwood and left-armer Bill Voce which had been terrorising batting orders around the country. During the course of the match Percy Fender and Nottinghamshire captain Arthur Carr, former England teammates on the 1923 tour of South Africa, got around to discussing the topic of Bradman and his alleged issues with fast, short-pitched bowling. Fender suggested Jardine

Harold Larwood.

would be interested in hearing any theories that Carr, Larwood and Voce might have and the men agreed to meet that night for dinner in the grill room at the Piccadilly Hotel.

In later years Larwood recalled that Jardine and Carr did most of the talking and that he and Voce sat quietly listening until asked their opinions. Jardine seemed to know a lot about the innings for someone who was not there but the film camera recording the event certainly was and he had meticulously studied every frame of it. Larwood's own recollection of events at The Oval in 1930 was outlined in his 1933 book *'Body-line?'* – a defence of what he alternatively termed 'Fast Leg Theory'. He recalled that after rain had fallen during the Australian innings, "[t]he ball was "popping"...Archie Jackson stood up to me, getting pinked once or twice in the process, and he never flinched. With Bradman it was different. It was because of that difference that I determined, then and there, that if I was again honoured with an invitation to go to Australia I would not forget that difference".

Jardine discussed the tactic of 'leg-theory' which was relatively common practice in county cricket where bowlers concentrated their line on or outside the leg-stump with a formation of fielders on the leg-side in an attempt to limit offside strokes and stifle scoring. The Nottinghamshire quick recalled in his 1963 biography *The Larwood Story* that Jardine asked him, "if I thought I could bowl on the leg stump making the ball come up at the body all the time so that Bradman had to play his shots to leg. 'Yes, I think that can be done'". Larwood confessed to having a "score to settle" with Bradman and Jardine said that if the tactic of Fast Leg Theory was successful on Bradman it might be expanded to include the rest of the Australian batsmen.

As if a wind of change was blowing through the 'gentleman's game' in England, a late-season match between Surrey and Yorkshire in August 1932 became embroiled in controversy and would foreshadow events in Australia later in the year. In the Surrey first innings, the reputable batting line-up of Jack Hobbs, Andy Sandham, Freddie Brown, Percy Fender and Douglas Jardine faced an intense and sustained bouncer barrage from tall, blonde, bespectacled fast bowler Bill Bowes. Twenty-thousand South Londoners who had packed The Oval howled derision at the Northern seamer. Forty-nine year-old Jack Hobbs, who had been also struggling with the heat, remonstrated with Bowes and the Yorkshire team about the danger of the tactics. The London *Times* was condemnatory of Bowes saying, "Hobbs must have wondered what sort of cricket he was playing. Bowes surely is not such a bad bowler as to rely on such feeble devices which are unworthy of the traditions of a great side" while the *Daily Mail* took an opposing view criticising Hobbs patting half-way down the pitch with his bat as if to mock the bowling, as an "unworthy" gesture. After making 90 runs opening the innings, Hobbs confided to reporters, "I didn't accuse Bowes of unfairness, but emphasised the danger. No tempers were lost". Jardine's answer to Yorkshire was stodgy defence which drew the ire of his own crowd. The captain was repeatedly booed by the Surrey fans as he stonewalled the bowling and his wicket was cheered when he was bowled on 35 by part-timer Maurice Leyland. In the end, Yorkshire won the match by 3 wickets and Bowes boasted the impressive figures of 10 for 135 effectively bowling himself onto the boat to Australia.

The Englishmen did not unveil the Fast Leg Theory tactic in Perth against the Western Australian and Combined Team sides. The opening leg of the tour was largely uneventful apart from the tourist's batting looking ominous with two centuries from the Nawab of Pataudi and one from Herbert Sutcliffe. Bradman underwhelmed the West Australian crowds who flocked to the W.A.C.A. ground only to see him score 3 runs.

Back in Sydney, Oldfield was throwing himself into his business before the cricket season got into full-swing. Despite being in the grip of the Great Depression he chose to invest in expanding his Hunter Street business with additions made to the premises. New South Wales Cricket Association president A.W. Green formally opened the extensions on 4 November 1932 saying that no man was more liked than Oldfield and that customers would receive as fair a deal as he gave his rivals on the field. Also in attendance at the opening was former Australian cricket captain, Monty Noble. Not known for mincing his words, Noble wished Oldfield the best of luck and said the wicket-keeper-businessman, "was plucky to make a plunge when men less game than he were moaning about tough times". Sentiments which drew applause from attendees.

As the English tourists made their way across the continent playing tour matches against South Australia and Victoria, Oldfield declined an invitation to play in an Australian XI match against them at the Melbourne Cricket Ground, preferring to play the Sheffield Shield match in Brisbane. Oldfield admitted he may have accepted the offer if Victorian left-arm wrist spinner Leslie Fleetwood-Smith had been playing to experience keeping to a bowling style he was unaccustomed to should he eventually make Test selection.

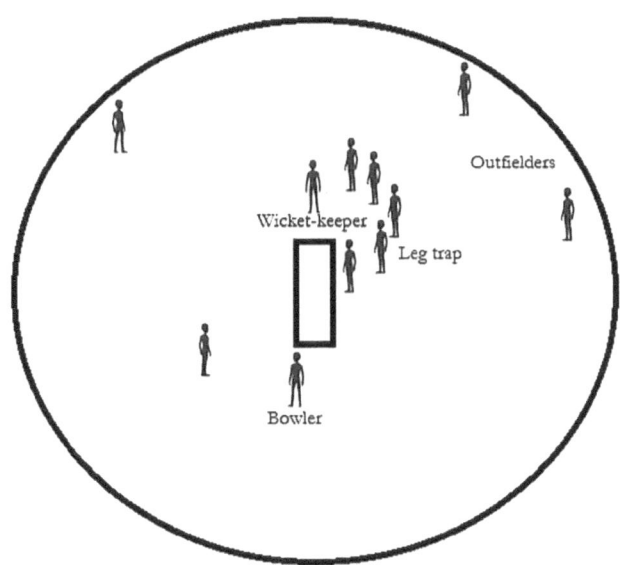

A typical Fast Leg Theory or 'Bodyline' field.

Preferring to go trout fishing, Jardine passed-on the captaincy reins to his deputy Bob Wyatt in the Australian XI match. England had made 282 and in the Australian XI's first innings Wyatt fired the bullets handed to him ordering an inner-ring of fielders on the leg side with outfielders in the deep to the eager Larwood, Voce and Bowes. With his tendency to be anchored to the crease, Australian captain Bill Woodfull was a stationary target for Larwood who pounded him in the heart with a painful blow. Bradman responded to the onslaught by adapting his footwork to the leg-side line and short length and improvising his stroke-play. The press jokingly dubbed it as "Russian Dancing", but it looked desperate and frantic- not what crowds had come to expect from the world record batsman. Larwood took Bradman's wicket in both innings: leg-before for 36 and bowled for 13 as he backed away tentatively. Despite the game ending in a draw, the solitary hope for Australia came in the 6-foot 6-inch form of Victorian seamer Lisle Nagel who obliterated the England batting by taking 8 for 32 in their second innings of 60, earning him selection for the first Test.

Bradman was the only New South Welshman to play in the Australian XI match and warned his teammates of what to expect upon his return to Sydney. It would not be long before Oldfield got to see the tactics up-close in the New South Wales tour match at the Sydney Cricket Ground. Jack Fingleton and Wendell Bill opened the account in front of a crowd of 26,000 for the royal blues against a side with Jardine returning as captain and Larwood resting. Resorting to Fast Leg Theory, Bill Voce dug the ball in short with a packed leg-side field hitting batsmen in the chest. Veteran medium-fast bowler Maurice Tate ditched line and length and bent his back a little more, striking opponents on the hipbone. Bradman came to the crease after Bill was dismissed for 22, but spent most of his innings ducking and weaving before falling L.B.W. to Tate for 18. A dour Fingleton was getting pulverised by Voce but was hanging on commendably when his captain Alan Kippax came and went for 3, another Tate victim. Stan McCabe arrived at the crease and immediately stabilised the situation with Fingleton, both combining in a 118-run partnership for the fourth wicket. England's Gubby Allen rounded-off the tail taking 5 for 69 including Oldfield (5) in the home side's first innings of 273.

The 1932-33 New South Wales Cricket Team: (standing l to r) Frank Cummins, Bill Brown, Gordon Stewart, Bill O'Reilly, Wendell Bill, Stan McCabe, Alec Marks (seated l to r) Bill Howell, Jack Fingleton, Alan Kippax, Ted Tyler, Bert Oldfield, Sid Hird. Absent: Don Bradman.

That night Oldfield came down with the flu virus and played no further part in the match – Hammy Love substituting as keeper with Jardine's consent despite not being named 12th man for the match. The start of the first Test in the following week raised realistic concerns that Oldfield would not be fit in time. England defeated New South Wales by an innings and 44 runs, demonstrating that the tourists were in threatening form with both bat and ball going into the 1932-33 Ashes series.

BODYLINE

Medically cleared to play after his bout of flu, Oldfield spoke to a journalist from the Sydney *Sun* on the eve of the first Test at his home in leafy Killara. "We don't know anything about this kind of bowling", he told the reporter, "and it's going to be very awkward. It's not doing the game any good because it intimidates the batsman and slows up the game". With infant daughters not old enough to be embarrassed, the 38-year-old keeper no doubt looked a sight, shadow-batting in his dressing gown to illustrate his misgivings about England's new bowling tactic.

"With a ball coming on the off (and here Oldfield played an imaginary cover drive), the batsman can place it there, there or there...[b]ut with it flying past here (indicating the left shoulder), the batsman has to play a blind shot, and he doesn't know where it's going". Asked if he had thought of a way to combat the tactic, Oldfield confessed he had not, saying, "it will be new to me...but I think the best thing to do would be to let those balls on the leg go by. Pick up the right balls to hit, and wait until you get up the other end".

In the face of England's in-form batting line-up and threatening new bowling tactic, the Australian Cricket Team looked far from a formidable unit prior to the first Test. After catching the same strain of the flu as Oldfield, Bradman advised the press that he felt fully recovered and expected to play. Bill Ponsford had not played cricket in almost a month after injuring his ankle in a Shield match against South Australia. It was not only physical niggles which plagued some of the team of whom had already faced England's Fast Leg Theory in the tour matches, such as Bill Woodfull who had been struck over the heart in the Australian XI game – as much a mental blow as a bodily one. The elegant stylist Alan Kippax had been injured twice the previous year attempting to hook bouncers. Weeks before getting hit in the head in the 1931-32 Shield opener against Queensland, he was playing against Parkes on a N.S.W. country tour when he mistimed a hook shot against a bouncer. Kippax suffered a broken nose and bruising to his right eye and had to withdraw completely from the tour that he was player-manager of to return to Sydney. Kippax's scores in the tour match against New South Wales in which the English employed Fast Leg Theory were an unconvincing 3 and 24.

Apart from a return to form from Bradman, the hopes for Australia were Fingleton, McCabe and Victor Richardson who was coming off 203 for South Australia in a recent Shield match. While expectations were always high for leg-spinners Grimmett and O'Reilly on the Bulli soil deck, the lanky pace pairing of Tim Wall and Lisle Nagel looked decidedly 'pop-gun' compared to their England counterparts.

A crowd of 35,000 basked in the midday sunshine of a cool fine Sydney Friday, many disappointed fans discussing the shock news that Bradman would not be playing the first Test. Examination by two doctors on the orders of the Board of Control found that the star batsman was lethargic and had a sore throat and would not be fit for cricket for up to a fortnight. Umpires George Borwick from New South Wales and South Australian George Hele were tasked to officiate in all five matches of the series. Both were fully aware of the English bowling tactic after its unveiling in the tour matches and had scanned the Laws of Cricket which confirmed that it was legal should any questions arise.

Australian captain Bill Woodfull facing Bodyline – note the leg trap in the foreground.

Liking what he saw of the Sydney Cricket Ground pitch, Woodfull won the toss and elected to bat, deciding to face the first ball of the series with his old partner Bill Ponsford at the other end. The pair confronted Larwood and Voce cautiously but confidently, only scoring two runs in the first ten overs. After the shine was taken off the ball, Jardine adopted variations of short-legs and a leg-trap of fielders to increasingly short-pitched bowling. Operating from the Randwick End, the left-handed Voce cut a shortish ball across Woodfull who edged it to keeper Les Ames for 7, the score 1 for 22.

Fingleton came to the crease to join Ponsford who seemed out-of-sorts, neither attacking or defending confidently, just fending the short balls away. Jardine continued to mix around his fields and change his bowlers, using all five in the first session. By lunch, Australia was 1 for 62, with Ponsford on 32 and Fingleton on 12. Immediately after the interval, having repeatedly ducked leg-side short balls from Larwood, Ponsford moved across his stumps to a fuller ball and was bowled attempting to glance without improving on his score.

Fingleton was joined by his New South Wales captain Alan Kippax who was struck on his left hand by a bouncer early in his innings. As if encountering an alien world, Kippax stood and watched incredulously as each ball of Voce's over flew high over his head. Generating searing pace, Larwood was finding his range in the second session and had Fingleton caught in the leg-trap by Allen at short-leg for 26. Uncharacteristically scratching-out an inelegant 8 runs, Kippax succumbed to a Larwood half-volley – adjudged leg-before-wicket.

The Australian first innings was on the verge of collapse at 4 for 87 with fresh batsmen Stan McCabe and Victor Richardson at the crease. The South Australian captain, known to be aggressive and good at playing the short ball, was struggling with Larwood's pace which was a significant step-up from Shield cricket. Richardson was struck twice in the leg requiring a stop in play to recover, but he and McCabe doggedly persisted and kept their wickets intact. Sensing that the stamina of the England bowlers was fading, the batting pair began to capitalise. Jardine may have felt control of the game slipping away and the Fast Leg Theory tactic faltering as McCabe and Richardson dominated the bowling over the course of two hours. Oldfield observed from the dressing room that the England captain was displaying "signs of perturbation". McCabe responded aggressively to the bouncer barrage pulling the ball forward through the inner-ring of fielders and hooking the ball backward of square-leg, often finding the pickets. Luck was with him as a top-edge off Larwood floated safely into the vacant slip region. As the after-work crowd swelled to 46,000, McCabe cracked a Voce no-ball to the leg boundary to bring up his century. At the taking of the new ball a rejuvenated England broke the partnership on 129 runs, Richardson having failed to middle a short ball from Voce, 1 run short of his half-century, falling to a catch taken by Hammond.

Oldfield arrived at the crease late in the day with the Australian innings on 5 for 216 to face a new ball still durable and deviating through the air and off the pitch. After scratching-out 4 runs off as many balls, a resurgent Larwood collected his edge and he was caught-behind. Of his brief experience, Oldfield admitted that, "facing the new form of attack, I found that it was a great deal more difficult than it appeared to be from the other side of the fence". Clarrie Grimmett held on until stumps and was on 17 at the end of the day. Stan McCabe had been the backbone of the innings scoring 127 of the team's 6 for 260. Despite England's fight-back at the end of Day 1, dissension in the ranks towards Jardine's tactics had become apparent with amateurs Gubby Allen refusing to bowl it and the Nawab of Pataudi refusing to field to it.

An incredible crowd of 58,058 Sydneysiders packed into the cricket ground for the second day of the Test hoping to see Stan McCabe rescue the Australian first innings. The right-hander from Grenfell did not disappoint and attacked the English bowling from the outset. Grimmett added only 2 to his overnight tally after being caught-behind off Voce. Now well into the tail, the enormous crowd's encouragement intensified, and sensing that the innings could quickly collapse, McCabe accelerated his scoring while his partners did their best to hang-on. His defiance and the crowd's passion seemed to impact the Englishmen psychologically with multiple mistakes creeping into their fielding effort. On 159, the cavalier McCabe cut the ball into the gully off Voce which Larwood dropped and when the Australian got to 170, Voce repaid Larwood in-kind by dropping a ball in the same position.

McCabe was stranded on 187 not out as Nagel, O'Reilly and Wall fell away with the score on 360. So significant was his performance that one of his many hook shots was immortalised in bronze decades later at the rear of the Sydney Cricket Ground's member's pavilion. The *Sydney Morning Herald* declared that, "McCabe's innings will go down in the annals of Test cricket as one of the finest ever played. Courage, skill, dash, and remarkable control marked the effort of this young batsman".

The adulation of the huge crowd was short-lived as the England top-order proved its quality against an ineffective Australian attack. Sutcliffe (194), Hammond (112) and the debutant Pataudi (102) conducted a leather hunt, methodically compiling an enormous total ending on 524. Oldfield featured in the very few highlights from the bowling side's perspective catching Maurice Leyland for a duck and taking a sharply rising edge off Jardine's bat keeping up to the stumps to McCabe's medium pace.

Behind 164 runs, Australia started their second innings feebly with Woodfull (0) and Ponsford (2) lost early. Jack Fingleton batted well with a resilient 40 to top score while Stan McCabe briefly showed his first innings brilliance by hooking Voce for six before falling to Hammond L.B.W. for 32. Showing no desire to hang around, Oldfield skied a bouncer off Larwood into the deep and was caught by Leyland for 1. At stumps on the fourth day the last Australian batting pair of Nagel and O'Reilly remained undefeated at the crease with a lead of only one run. In a farce only the game of cricket could produce, players significantly out-numbered spectators as they walked out onto a virtually-deserted, sun-drenched Sydney Cricket Ground, a lone figure sitting on The Hill a stark contrast to the clamouring multitude of Day 2. O'Reilly was quickly yorked by Voce without increasing the score. Requiring one run to win the first Test, vice-captain Bob Wyatt and Herbert Sutcliffe, his dark hair glistening with Brill Cream in the early afternoon light, strode to the crease. A push by Sutcliffe into the offside off McCabe's first ball concluded proceedings – England winning by 10 wickets.

Though the Test was arguably won by England's batsmen, the topic of conversation was still the old enemy's new bowling tactics. Reporting on the first Test, Hugh Buggy from the Melbourne *Herald* formed a compound word from colleague Jack Worrall's previous description that the English had started bowling "on the body line" and the expression 'Bodyline' was born. In a satirical article in the Sydney *Sun*, H.T.Cantwell wrote a fictional Test report where the scoring of the Australian batsman was measured in injuries. On the mock scoresheet, Oldfield's dismissal was listed as 'concussion'.

Apart from McCabe's extraordinary innings, the Australian team was not spared from criticism with glaring failures across the board. Woodfull and Kippax looked rattled in the face of the Bodyline tactic while Ponsford meekly fended at short balls or just allowed them to impact his body. McCabe, Fingleton and Richardson were the only batsmen seemingly able to show any resistance while Oldfield no longer looked like he could be counted upon to knock-out a typical innings of 20 or 30. Leg-spinner Grimmett fruitlessly toiled on the usually-conducive Sydney wicket while Wall and Nagel reflected the paucity of Australian pace bowling stocks.

Umpire George Hele recalled in his book *Bodyline Umpire*, that he and George Borwick, "were of the opinion that, if this attack continued, let alone intensified by application from both ends, somebody would be killed or seriously maimed during the remaining Tests. Borwick and I sensed this. The crowd sensed it and its demonstrations against this form of attack was, to my mind, utterly justified".

As the teams separated, Shield cricket resumed in the hopes some answers to Australia's problems could be found in the domestic competition. The Marylebone Cricket Club embarked on tour matches against Tasmania and the N.S.W. Southern Districts in Wagga Wagga where Douglas Jardine's reputed arrogance and contempt for Australians was on full display. In an expression of good will, the citizens of Wagga had organised a fundraising dance for bowler Maurice Tate's son Michael, who was born while his father was on tour. Jardine forbade any player, including Tate, from attending the event which carried-on regardless and raised £100 ($9900) for the newborn.

Oldfield travelled to Adelaide in mid-December for the match against South Australia where he improved on his batting form with 40 and 13 not out. To spend Judith's first Christmas with the family, he headed back to Sydney while the rest of the team travelled to Melbourne to play Victoria where Hammy Love filled-in in his place. Bradman returned in the match scoring 157 while Fingleton (85) and McCabe (48) continued their positive momentum.

With Bradman available for the second Test, the selectors also brought in Victorian left-hander Leo O'Brien, who had scored successive First-Class half-centuries, to make his Test debut.

Ponsford and Kippax failed to make a claim for selection with their opportunities in the Shield and were dropped while captain Woodfull who was equally unconvincing, retained his position. Bert Ironmonger replaced Victorian teammate Lisle Nagel who made himself unavailable for selection due to work commitments, thus ending his Test career. The ascendant English only made one change to the line-up substituting spinner Hedley Verity for seamer Bill Bowes. Jardine would be gambling all his chips on the Bodyline tactic.

Such was the public interest in the second Test that around 40,000 spectators were already in the Melbourne Cricket Ground an hour before the first day's play on 30 December 1932. First-aid crews were kept busy with scores of women and children fainting from the crush and the stifling heat as thousands more surged through the turnstiles on the sweltering Friday. Captains Woodfull and Jardine emerged from the shade of the Grey Smith Stand into the blinding light for the toss, won by Woodfull – Australia would bat.

The Australian top-order was in a stubborn mood, both against conventional fields and the Bodyline attack. While openers Fingleton and Woodfull were not dismissed, the scoring plodded along at a snail's pace. Play was punctuated with frustrating delays involving a faulty ball, Larwood's left boot malfunctioning and supplementary drinks breaks due to the heat. Allen broke through Woodfull's defences when he was on 10, bringing debutant Leo O'Brien to the crease for a baptism of fire. No longer troubled by footwear issues, Larwood dug in an effort-ball to O'Brien that seemed like it would decapitate him if not for his gloves deflecting the projectile at the last fraction of a second. After the lunch break, O'Brien had scratched out 10 runs before being run-out by keeper Ames attempting a quick single off Fingleton.

On 2 for 67 the stage was set for Don Bradman to save the day as the Melbourne Cricket Ground swelled to a world record crowd of 63,983 in the mid-afternoon. Striding through the wrought iron gate onto the vast green expanse, he passed press photographers to the adulation of the anticipating swarm. After what seemed like an endless walk, Bradman took guard at the Member's end to face Bowes. For Jardine, this would be the true test of his hypothesis, finally applying his theory to its intended target in the Test arena. Normally able to clear his mind and give the ball his undivided attention, Bradman could not shake a premonition that this would be a bouncer. It did not help that the English had made minor fielding changes on the leg-side – it was confirmation. Bowes shuffled in on his gangling run and pitched the ball halfway, but outside the off-stump. Bradman moved his backfoot to the off-side in anticipation but was followed there by the ball. Awkwardly unbalanced and committed to the hook, the ball got tangled near his bat handle and was slingshot onto his leg-stump. Bradman 0. Before the bails had landed, he had seamlessly switched the momentum from his botched hook-shot into a walk back to the pavilion. Bradman threw his head back and bathed his face in sunlight revealing a grimacing grin of incredulity and embarrassment.

Losing partners rapidly, Fingleton continued to display character beyond his brief Test experience in spite of getting struck in the ribs off Bowes and repeated blows to his hip and fingers from Larwood. The opener and his middle-order partners McCabe (32) and Richardson (34) capitalised on the tiring England bowlers until he was bowled middle stump by Allen for a valiant 83.

At 5 for 156, Oldfield joined Richardson in the middle-order resistance and anchored the partnership while the South Australian hunted for boundaries until he was caught (34) in the leg-trap with the score on 6 for 188. In fading light, as a summer

Don Bradman is bowled for 0 by Bill Bowes in the second Test at the Melbourne Cricket Ground.

storm brewed on the horizon, Oldfield and Grimmett fought to hold-on until stumps, but the spinner fended a ball to Sutcliffe in the leg-trap off Voce for 2 which brought an end to the first day.

On Day 2, Oldfield remained on 27 not out after batting with the tail to get the total to 228. The keeper again had the pleasure of snaring a Jardine edge as the English struggled against the spin of Bill O'Reilly (5 for 63) and Tim Wall's (4 for 52) swing and cutters. Herbert Sutcliffe had top-scored in the England first innings leaving the team on 9 for 161 with the dismissal of Voce for 6, leaving Allen not out for 26.

New Years Day 1933 fell on the Sabbath and was thus a rest day in the cricket but the Melbourne sporting public's fascination with the Test match did not take any respite. Spectators started gathering at the M.C.G. gates at dawn the next day in anticipation of the resumption of play at midday. In excess of 60,000 had surged into the ground by 10am resulting in the gates being closed and thousands turned away to avoid a repeat of the first day. The crowd only saw two overs of the England innings before the final wicket fell on 169 leaving a deficit of 59.

Opening the Australian second innings after encouraging applause from the capacity crowd, Fingleton would not repeat his heroics after nicking the ball with a tentative prod into Les Ames's gloves for 1. O'Brien joined Woodfull and the pair carefully compiled a partnership of 26 before O'Brien's off-stump was sent cartwheeling by a Larwood bullet for 11. Bradman arrived at the non-striker's end for the commencement of the new Bill Bowes over with Woodfull immediately taking a single off the first ball. Excited tension gripped the ground as he faced off against his first innings nemesis. Playing the short-of-a-length ball on its merits (this time), Bradman released the crowd's pent-up jubilation as he pulled Bowes to the mid-wicket boundary for 4. He continued to be the aggressor with his captain holding down the other end in a half-century partnership until Woodfull fell after a grafting 26. A delivery from Allen bowled new batsman Stan McCabe for a duck which brought Richardson to the crease with Australia on the verge of collapse at 4 for 81. Bradman continued to pull the ball savagely through gaps in the leg-side field forward of square-leg. McCabe in Sydney had defied the tactic, perhaps Bradman's first-ball duck was an aberration? Jardine must have been processing that Fast Leg Theory may require a return to the drawing board if the primary target continued to resist it in this fashion. Richardson scored quickly, including three boundaries, until he too was dismissed for 32 – L.B.W. to Hammond. Doing their best to support Bradman, who was battering the England attack, the tail continued to disintegrate. Oldfield (6) and Grimmett (0) came and went, both bowled by Voce while Wall (3) and O'Reilly (0) were victims of Hammond.

Much like the late-afternoon light, hope of a century seemed to be fading for Bradman stranded on 98 as 50-year-old batting bunny Bert Ironmonger walked to the crease to face the remaining two balls from Hammond's over. As the big Queenslander-cum-Victorian passed his junior, he assured him, "don't worry son, I won't let you down". To the relief of everyone bar the touring Englishmen – he survived. Voce's first ball was waist-high and punched by Bradman through mid-wicket. The leather was chased by Bill Bowes from mid-on but he could not haul it in before the pair had run 3 and Bradman arrived at triple-figures. The adulation continued soon after as a lumbering Ironmonger was run out for 0 and the Australian innings closed on 191 setting England 251 runs for victory. The centurion was cheered by tens-of-thousands of jovial Melburnians for his 103 not out, running off the field as his opponents politely clapped their acknowledgement.

By the end of Day 3, the England openers started the run chase confidently getting to stumps at 43 without loss. Early the next day a batting collapse was sparked when Sutcliffe was bowled by O'Reilly with ball pitching on middle and hitting the top of off-stump, having not added to his overnight total of 33. Oldfield believed that much of the subsequent collapse was psychological owing to Sutcliffe's statement to his teammates upon entering the dressing room that the ball had "spun a yard". Of the string of tentative batsmen that arrived at the crease, Oldfield confessed that, "I am convinced that Sutcliffe's remark…was of immense benefit to Australia".

On a dry wicket with some deteriorating patches, the spinning pair of O'Reilly (5 for 66) and Ironmonger (4 for 26) dismantled the

England batting order to have them dismissed for 139. Australia's 111 run victory levelled the 1932-33 Ashes series one apiece, and at this point both teams' contrasting strengths and weaknesses became apparent. While Australia's potency was in the middle-order batsmen and spinners, England's was in their strong top-order and fast men. In the press, Oldfield credited the bowlers as the key to Australia's success. With the series on a knife-edge both captains went into the third Test at the Adelaide Oval pondering the way forward to force an advantage in the arm-wrestle while no doubt dwelling on their own personal lack of form.

THE BATTLE OF ADELAIDE

The dramatic and controversial 1932-33 Ashes series rolled into the genteel South Australian capital of orderly streets, parklands and churches. The event that had already generated record crowds looked set to grip the city, with booked-out hotels and the stock exchange closing for Day 1 of the Test in anticipation of a distracted populace.

The pretty, elongated oval enclosed by amber-roofed grandstands and Moreton Bay figs at the Cathedral End would become the focus of the deadlocked contest. The overwhelming public attention was reflected in the intense media interest with journalists and photographers clambering for scoops and vantage points. Adelaide radio 5CL's ball-by-ball coverage would be relayed nationally and newsreel cameras would also be fixed on the action. The two major newsreel services covering the Adelaide Test match were Pathe News and British Movietone.

Prior to arriving in Adelaide, the hitherto-unpopular Jardine made remarks that the regional Bendigo pitch he played on for a tour match was far superior to the one prepared for the second Test at the hallowed Melbourne Cricket Ground, where his team had lost. The England captain further aggravated Adelaide

Douglas Jardine

locals by insisting they be locked-out of the tourist's pre-match net session. Under pressure to moderate his Fast Leg Theory tactics and diversify his attack, Jardine substituted spinner Verity for Bowes and replaced conscientious objector Pataudi for Lancastrian left-hand batsman, Eddie Paynter.

The only change the Australian selectors would make in their winning side would be swapping Leo O'Brien for Bill Ponsford who had been 12th man for the Melbourne Test. Since the first Test, Ponsford had only made 12 and 24 in two Sheffield Shield matches for Victoria and was evidently selected on hopes and wishes and not solid batting form. Not known for his nimble footwork, the

Victorian was a stationary target for the England attack. To combat the tactic, Ponsford's response was to improvise padding beneath his shirt to cover the left-side of his back. He would turn his head and absorb the blow rather than defend his body with his bat and risk being caught by the inner-ring of fielders. For Australian batsman increasingly devising ways to mitigate bodily injury, it may have seemed that they were no longer participating in a sport.

Adelaide Oval curator Alby Wright claimed he had produced his best pitch at the venue in 14 years which Jardine decided to bat on after winning the toss. The English were in early strife at 4 for 30 with the second Test trio of Wall, O'Reilly and Ironmonger back in threatening form. The batting side resorted to niggling tactics: Jardine complaining that Richardson was distracting the batsmen by moving in the field and Leyland being forced to apologise for an allegation that Ironmonger was using resin on the ball. The initial joy for the Australians was short-lived as the middle-order of Leyland (83), Wyatt (78) and Paynter (77) stabilised the innings which ended on 341, midway through the second day.

Australian openers Woodfull and Fingleton walked out onto the Adelaide Oval to the applause of a staggering record crowd of 50,962 spectators. Almost one-sixth of the population of Adelaide was concentrated into those few acres of the city on Saturday, 14 January 1933. In the warm afternoon, boundary pickets were used as coat-racks by barrackers as Woodfull took guard at the River End. Gubby Allen strayed onto the leg-stump with the new ball and Woodfull capably clipped him to square-leg for a single. Awkwardly playing from the backfoot and prodding unconvincingly at the ball, Fingleton edged to Ames for a duck – Australia 1 for 1.

Bradman came to the wicket and saw-off the remaining balls of Allen's over as Woodfull prepared to face Larwood at the other end. Bowling to a conventional field but for a seemingly

Australian captain Bill Woodfull struck over the heart by a delivery from Harold Larwood.

ever-present short-leg, Larwood was in faultless rhythm and was generating extreme pace. On the final delivery, he pitched the ball short of a length on middle-stump, as Woodfull jumped to attempt to get over the top of the ball it crashed over his heart with a sickening thud. The batsman dropped his bat and clutched at his chest walking to the offside rocking forward and back in agony. Woodfull doubled over as English fielders and his batting partner ran to assist, hands hurriedly propping him up as his knees briefly buckled. Seemingly unconcerned, Larwood turned and retrieved his cap from the umpire. A brooding crowd, undoubtedly equating any short-pitched delivery as the notorious 'Bodyline' bowling they had been absorbing in the press, erupted angrily as their beloved captain attempted to regain his composure. Out in the centre, with his cap now retrieved, Larwood approached the group of England players surrounding Woodfull and Bradman in the area of silly-point. Watching over proceedings and possibly sensing blood in the water, Jardine complimented his approaching spearhead, "well bowled, Harold" within earshot of the batsmen. Either through competitive instinct, or perhaps a student of Sun Tzu's *Art of War* observation, "[a] whole army may be robbed of its spirit; a commander-in-chief may be robbed of his presence of mind" – the England captain knew his opposite number being taken down could initiate the domino effect on the rest of the team.

At the commencement of Larwood's next over, Jardine further applied the figurative foot-to-the-throat, when at the bowler's request he authorised a Bodyline field with the ball only three overs old. The fast bowler obliged by pounding a rib-high delivery at the groggily tentative Woodfull, who once again jumped in the air only to have the bat knocked from his hands and the ball falling just short of the inner fielders. Of the incident, Jardine wrote in his book *In Quest of the Ashes*, "[h]ad either [Larwood] or I realised the misinterpretation to which we were to be subjected, neither of us would have set that particular field". While not clarifying what his and Larwood's true intentions were, Jardine further attempted to vindicate himself by blaming Woodfull for choosing to stay on the field if he was unwell, rather than retire hurt.

A single brought Bradman to the Cathedral End to face the onslaught, but unlike the waist high balls he dispatched at Melbourne off a docile pitch, he was ducking under seemingly insurmountable head-high projectiles. A fuller ball from Larwood saw Bradman defending his hip and the ball popped-up into the hands of Allen at short-leg for 8 runs. Felled by a textbook Bodyline delivery, the star batsman tucked his bat under his arm and removed his gloves to the disappointed groans of the deflated crowd. Bewildered and perhaps lost in thought, Bradman walked to the mid-wicket boundary only to find that he had missed the gate by a pitch-length and waddled embarrassed along the fence-line to access the refuge of the dressing-room. The Sydney Test was now a distant memory, as McCabe meekly fell identically to Bradman for the same score, this time Jardine snaring the catch- Australia 3 for 34.

The re-called Bill Ponsford joined his battered old partner to face a beating of his own as he applied his risk-averse strategy with a torso swathed in padding. Ponsford pounced on any loose opportunities either side of the wicket by targeting the slim Adelaide Oval square boundaries with pull and cut shots. Woodfull doggedly assembled 22 in his 17-run partnership with Ponsford before he was bowled by Allen, gauntly shuffling back to the pavilion away from the ordeal.

After emerging from the dressing room showers, Woodfull became engaged in an infamous exchange with England manager Plum Warner and co-manager Dick Palairet after the pair had entered the Australian dressing room to enquire about his injury. Standing with a towel around his waist and a bruise developing on his chest, Woodfull sternly addressed his visitor, "I don't want to see you Mr Warner. There are two teams out there. One is trying to play cricket and the other is not". With their conciliatory gesture firmly rebuked, the pair silently turned and left. Much of the revisionist history of Bodyline has implied that Woodfull's response may have been impulsive or hyperbolic. If not for the injury itself, admittedly received from a non-Bodyline delivery, but for Jardine's subsequent compliment to Larwood and Bodyline field placing to capitalise on his injury, Woodfull was in no mood to be placatory. For the son of a Methodist minister, aware of Christ's exhortation to "turn the other cheek" when struck by one's enemy, Woodfull would not entertain the notion of stooping to retaliate.

As the shadows lengthened on a brutal day, Richardson had made a decent start as he had done in every other innings of the series. He survived until stumps on 21 not out with Ponsford undefeated on 45 and Australia on 4 for 109. A Sunday rest day came to the rescue as a welcome relief to the oppressive ugliness that had engulfed the normally friendly-confines of the Adelaide Oval.

On Day 3 of the third Test, Monday 16 January 1933, a crowd of 32,527 spectators filed into the Adelaide Oval with hopes that Ponsford and local hero Richardson would continue the fight-back. Disappointingly, Richardson under-edged a pull shot off Allen into his stumps after adding only 7 to his personal tally. With the run-chase hanging precariously at 5 for 131, Oldfield arrived at the crease. Ponsford kept batting pugnaciously as he compiled runs and bruises. The wicket-keeper, who had prided himself on his batting, had been in questionable form for the whole season but fed off the resilience being shown by his partner. By lunch, the pair had reached their 50-run partnership milestone in 59 minutes and taken the total to 181. Entering the pavilion, Ponsford was on 80 and Oldfield was on 26 with a couple of boundaries under his belt. Shortly after the break, the valiant innings of Ponsford came to an end on 85 as he tried to turn a Voce ball to leg and it bowled him with the score now 6 for 194. His bruise tally was assessed in the dressing room at a dozen with Larwood responsible for about nine of them. Ponsford would make himself unavailable for district cricket upon his return to Melbourne on account of the extent of the bruising.

Noticeable throughout the day was a brooding undercurrent of hostility from the crowd towards the English, flaring-up particularly when fielders chased a ball in the outfield only to receive a torrent of jeering and abuse. Grimmett had now joined Oldfield in the middle and the duo pushed the total past 200, still 141 runs short of the England first innings. The South Australian leg-spinner became a victim of the new ball after compiling 10 runs and was replaced by his state teammate Tim Wall with the score 7 for 212.

Oldfield had reached the high-30s in a spirited innings that, despite the incursion well into the Australian tail-order, remained an irritation to Jardine and Larwood. Facing Larwood, coming in from the River End, he glanced a thigh-high ball through the gap between the leg-slip and gully to the boundary for his fourth four. Having taken off for a run, Oldfield had reached the non-striker's end as Umpire Hele signalled the boundary. Returning to the Cathedral End, the keeper cheekily addressed the bowler who stood motionless and unresponsive at the end of his follow-through – hands on hips. Larwood started pitching the ball shorter hoping for a better result. Throughout his two-hour innings, Oldfield had been experiencing trouble sighting Larwood's deliveries due to an inadequately small sight-screen at the River End and the activity of patrons around it. One delivery had him in the air, fending-off a head-high ball that ballooned short of the slips on the off-side, which frantically had him looking around to see if he had been caught.

Oldfield now on 41 and the score on 7 for 218, the fastest bowler in the world Harold Larwood once again commenced his long rhythmic run – his foot hitting the crease like a striking hammer. The ball pitched short of a length but Oldfield found himself in an awkward position to deal with it. With his weight forward on the front foot, he had committed to a cross-batted shot but the ball was onto him too quickly. As he rocked onto his back leg swivelling through the stroke, his horizontal bat cut the air aimlessly in front of him – missing the ball that impacted with his right temple on the junction of his Baggy Green cap. The crack was audible to everyone in the ground.

The momentum of the shot swung Oldfield around, his gloved

Bert Oldfield is struck in the head by a delivery from Harold Larwood. George Borwick is the square-leg umpire, England's George 'Gubby' Allen is the short-leg fielder.

hands discarding the bat almost hitting the stumps which he had been defending a fraction of a second before. In his follow-through, Larwood raised his right hand, mouth agape at what was unfolding before him as the ball rebounded at pace off Oldfield's skull out towards the regulation cover-point position. Stumbling to the off-side Oldfield clutched at his head, his cap coming off in his hands then reflexively restored in an effort to brace the pain as he slumped to the ground propped shakily on an elbow, reclining on his right side.

Non-striker batsman Tim Wall, umpire George Hele, short-leg fielder Gubby Allen and Larwood were the first to get to Oldfield as the Adelaide Oval crowd exploded in uproar beyond the pickets. According to George Hele in his book *Bodyline Umpire*, Oldfield was bleeding from where he was struck and was "in no condition to speak". While still on the ground suffering from a traumatic

A different angle of the ball striking Oldfield in the temple and ricocheting away.

head injury, Larwood claimed Oldfield had accepted fault for his predicament which the bowler would frequently cite in his defence well into the future.

Gubby Allen ran into the full force of the unbridled rage and abuse emanating from the grandstand to fetch a towel and water while his compatriots huddled in the pitch-square as police officers in black tunics and white helmets filed along the boundary. From within the grandstand a telephone call was made from the South Australian Cricket Association offices to police headquarters for reinforcements. Excusing himself from the Governor of South Australia's viewing box, a besuited Bill Woodfull strode onto the grassed playing area with a headmaster's authority. Having had his cut bathed with the water, Oldfield rose to his feet after five minutes which momentarily pacified the crowd making use of the towel to wipe the remaining blood and sweat from his forehead. Woodfull retrieved his bat and the jug of water and escorted his wicket-keeper off the field to rapturous applause, but once he reached the dressing room, he collapsed.

After a lengthy delay, number 10 batsman Bill O'Reilly struggled through the baying mob as he descended the grandstand steps. Larwood now became the focal point of fury as Adelaide's *The News* recorded that, "[t]he crowd for a time lost all interest in the Australian innings, and concentrated on howling at the fast bowler. Meanwhile Oldfield reeled around in the Australian dressing room [floor], dazed and unable to say clearly what happened". Discussion amongst the Australian players concentrated on whether he had edged the ball or not, but "Oldfield was far too sick to clear-up the point". The general consensus of the dressing room was that there was no deflection involved. Once in a position to pass comment on the series in March 1933, umpire George Hele wrote in a column in the Adelaide *Advertiser* saying that the delivery was a genuine 'bumper' and that Oldfield did not make contact with it.

As interstate players often had to supply their own board and lodging during Test matches in the 1930s, Oldfield had fortuitously organised to stay at the home of general practitioner Dr Kenneth Steele in the seaside suburb of Glenelg. Still on the floor of the dressing room, Australian selector and medical doctor Charles Dolling examined Oldfield who was sporting an egg-sized lump over his right temple and saying that he was struggling to focus his eyes properly. Dolling passed-on his observations and placed the stricken keeper into the hands of ambulance officers who drove him out to Dr Steele's residence.

Bill O'Reilly took guard at the crease for the remainder of the over in what seemed to have become more of a gladiatorial contest than a game of cricket, where scoring runs no longer seemed to be the relevant consideration. On the verge of a riot, Larwood continued plying his trade as his run-up was counted-out by the crowd in an attempt to break his rhythm – "five, four, three, two, one…ya bastard!". At the suggestion of their captain to not put themselves at any further risk, the Australian tail offered no resistance and the innings finished on 222.

The Adelaide Oval crowd had settled down considerably over the innings break, maintaining a menacing watchfulness over the arena. Virtual silence met England openers Sutcliffe and Jardine as they came to the crease. Representative baseballer Victor Richardson took possession of the gloves for the unenviable task of keeping up to the stumps to Australia's spinning trio: Grimmett, Ironmonger and O'Reilly. Apart from substitute fieldsman Leo O'Brien snaring Sutcliffe off Tim Wall for 7, which inspired a release of applause, the atmosphere was dour until stumps was called with England on 1 for 85.

While Oldfield recuperated under the watchful eye of his host, the political turmoil resulting from his injury was in the early stages of fermentation. Adelaide-based president of the Australian Board of Control for Cricket, Bernard Scrymgour had witnessed the day's events from the stands and was moved to contact his fellow board members regarding the crisis. The Board agreed that an approach be made towards the English management with a request to cease the 'body-bowling' tactic. The appeal was unsuccessful as Plum Warner and Dick Palairet advised they were powerless to influence on-field tactics which was the jurisdiction of the team captain Douglas Jardine. With that approach ineffective, urgent Board officials conferred and came to the agreement that a cable should be sent to the Marylebone Cricket Club to address the issue. Bill Jeanes, Board secretary and another South Australian present during the Test match, rang around state delegates who confirmed the following wording:-

> 'Body-line bowling assumed such proportions as to menace best interests of the game, making protection of the body the main consideration. Causing intensely bitter feeling between players, as well as injury. In our opinion is unsportsmanlike. Unless stopped at once likely to upset friendly relations existing between Australia and England'.

The off-field shots were fired.

WAS OLDFIELD FACING BODYLINE?

OVER THE YEARS, THE assertion that neither Bill Woodfull or Bert Oldfield were struck by Bodyline deliveries, has gained traction – the implication being that Australian players, administrators and crowds had overreacted in blaming the tactic on those key incidents.

Based on the film and photographic evidence, Bill Woodfull was batting to a relatively orthodox field when struck over the heart by Larwood. While a short-leg and short mid-on were in place, there appeared to be a conventional slip, a gully and a point positioned on the offside. With there being no fielders close-in behind square on the legside, it can be concluded that Woodfull was not facing Bodyline when impacted by the ball.

The Bodyline strategy however, was not static once it was employed. Jardine constantly shifted his fielders like chess pieces in accordance with how he read the flow of play – up to six fielders were photographed close-in around the batsman. An inner 'leg-trap', outfielders on the leg boundary and sweepers on the off were the broad brushstrokes of the Bodyline field – Jardine commanded the palette.

Journalist Hugh Buggy, writing for Adelaide's *The News* in the

evening edition of 16 January 1933, observed the following:-
"Larwood had sought to lure Oldfield into the Allen short-leg trap. He dropped one down just short of the fieldsman. The next ball rose high. Oldfield swung his bat at it, and then recoiled away from the wicket. It looked as if the ball flew off the edge of the bat, and struck Oldfield in the head".

The following day in the News Limited affiliate paper, Broken Hill's *Barrier Miner*, additional text of Buggy's eyewitness account immediately preceding his *The News* version was included:-
'Larwood had moved the field across to the leg side now for Oldfield, who was 41, and two balls tore past his shoulder'.

It can be established from Buggy's observations that Jardine and Larwood had maintained the common practice of reverting to Bodyline, from orthodox off-stump tactic, once the shine was taken off the ball – in this case – the second new ball. According to Buggy, the first two balls of Larwood's over were shoulder-high bouncers in the line of, or outside leg stump, which passed through to keeper Les Ames, while the third ball was directed at Oldfield's body and was safely negotiated – falling in-front of short-leg.

British Movietone positioned a camera in the Mostyn Evan Stand on the north-western side of the ground, while Pathe News had two cameras: one side-on in the George Giffen Stand, which housed the members and players areas, and another atop the iconic 1911 Adelaide Oval scoreboard at the north-eastern side. The Movietone camera, in the elevated position above the third-man boundary, has become the 'Zapruder' film of the dramatic Adelaide Test incidents involving Oldfield and Woodfull. While the Movietone footage captures the moment in explicit detail, valuable information and context can be gleaned by the other films, much like the additional recordings captured in Dealey Plaza on 22 November 1963 – the assassination of U.S. president John F. Kennedy.

The view of Oldfield being struck in the head from the top of the Adelaide scoreboard. In place is a 3-man leg trap and a short mid-on.

The Pathe motion picture camera on top of the scoreboard, as well as a separate press photographer, documented the field-placings employed by Jardine and Larwood. Surrounding Oldfield on the leg-side was an inner-trap including Gubby Allen at short-leg and unknown fielders at leg gully and a wide leg-slip. In addition to the leg-trap was the unusual field placing of a short mid-on in line with the popping crease. While the Pathe footage clips the moment of impact with Oldfield, it depicts players and umpires rushing to the stricken batsman – with the last few frames revealing a fielder walking in from a deep backward square leg position. It can be confirmed from photographic and film sources that there was at least a majority of five fielders on the leg-side with a gully and cover-point on the off-side, leaving two fielders unaccounted for due to the limitations of camera angles from the day.

While entirely within the Laws of Cricket at the time, Oldfield was facing what would be an unlawful suite of bowling tactics today. In 1957, laws were changed to limit two fielders behind square on the leg-side; in Adelaide at least three England players were placed behind square (leg gully, leg slip, deep backward square-leg). Hugh Buggy's account indicates that Oldfield was struck on the fourth successive bouncer of the Larwood over. While he claims that, "[it] looked as if the ball flew off the edge of the bat", Oldfield never confirmed that he had top-edged the ball and Umpire Hele said there was no edge from his vantage point. In 1994, the International Cricket Council legislated a restriction in Test cricket of two bouncers per over. Whether umpires would have stepped-in, empowered with the discretion to judge intimidatory intent taking into account Oldfield's batting ability, is a matter of conjecture.

The lack of a slip cordon and a majority leg-side field indicate that the England Cricket Team had changed from conventional off-stump tactics to a leg-side strategy. Larwood had bowled three bouncers around the line of leg-stump in an attempt to lure Oldfield into defending a ball into the clutches of the leg-trap or hooking a catch into the deep, and while short-pitched, the fourth ball was closer to a middle-stump line which Oldfield lost sight of. Based on the available evidence, it appears Oldfield was facing a modified form of the Fast Leg Theory tactic when struck in the head.

THE WOUNDED WARRIOR

AFTER A NIGHT'S SLEEP, Oldfield awoke at the home of Dr Steele with reduced swelling of his temple wound, but a subconjunctival haemorrhage of the right eye (a discolouration as a result of the head trauma) was starting to develop. Still feeling the effects of the concussion from the day before, Oldfield reported a vertigo sensation when on his feet. Guided by medical advice, he would not be taking the field at the Adelaide Oval.

Back in Sydney, Ruth had received a telegram from Douglas Jardine expressing regret on behalf of the England team at the "unfortunate accident" that had befallen her husband. The worried wife told the press that she wanted to talk Bert out of playing cricket: "It does not seem like a game...it is more like a battle", she told reporters. Soon after, Mrs Oldfield answered the front door to accept the delivery of twin Shirley Temple dolls for the girls sent on behalf of Jardine.

Following an x-ray it was confirmed that Oldfield had sustained a linear fracture of the right frontal bone of the skull. Assuring the family and the cricketing public that there was no need for any further concern, Dr Steele advised that he needed time for the fracture to 'knit' and that he may be out for the rest of the season as a result.

As the Test match continued, Jardine shuffled the England batting order which the Australian bowlers struggled to dislodge after the initial success of breaking the opening partnership. Bill O'Reilly took his marathon over tally to 100 for the match with his 4 for 97 off 50 followed by Ironmonger with 3 for 87 off 57 overs in the England innings of 412. Set an unlikely 531 runs to win and down a batsman, Australia resumed the sixth and final day of the Test on 4 for 120 in front of a smattering of fans. His right temple covered in sticking plaster, Oldfield was well enough to watch Woodfull carry his bat for 73 from the stands. He was in a conciliatory mood saying, "[i]t was simply bad luck that I was hit" and did not apportion blame to Larwood or the English for what happened. Oldfield said that he recalled the ball breaking from the off which made him misjudge its flight before hitting him. After witnessing Australia's 338 run defeat, he boarded the train that night for Sydney, via Melbourne.

A relieved Ruth Oldfield was waiting at Central Station for her husband's return home. The reunited couple were captured by a *Sydney Morning Herald* photographer arm-in-arm and smiling before getting into a waiting vehicle. Settling at home, Oldfield was interviewed by former First-Class cricketer and cricket writer A.G. 'Johnnie' Moyes for the Sydney *Sun* of 22 January 1933. The keeper was more forthright than his previously pacifying tone. "I am totally opposed to the body-line bowling with the packed leg field of 4 or 5 men close in and two on the fence...[i]t is not only dangerous but it is definitely prejudicial to the best interests of the game of cricket".

Outlining his recollection of the Adelaide incident, he said:-

'The ball which hit me pitched on the line of the wicket. I lost it and it hit me. Previously I had been ducking to dodge

Larwood's fliers and have no doubt that my knock was indirectly caused by the leg field tactics. One has to be so careful with the field placed in that way. Larwood's pace is such that a batsman must in a split-second make up his mind what shot to play, or whether to play one, or to duck. The ball may swing in to the body, it may come stump high or it may fly, and with all those things to consider it is a most difficult job to defend without being caught. And in the middle of it all I lost sight of the ball, and to that extent must not blame anyone else'.

Oldfield would not be drawn into the cable controversy that his injury had sparked but declared his admiration for his captain Bill Woodfull of whom he said his, "admiration grows daily". Responding to the many reports speculating that he may be out for the remainder of the season, Oldfield confessed, "I feel all right" but admitted his fate was in the hands of the doctors. The family posed for the press cameras with the patriarch still sporting a bandaged forehead. Sitting in a velvet armchair in the lounge room of 'Poitiers', Oldfield nursed his cherished girls, Ruth Mary now 3-years-old and Judith Ann, 9 months – the latter startled by the camera flash.

On 23 January 1933, the Marylebone Cricket Club committee released its response to the Australian cable:-

'We, Marylebone Cricket Club, deplore your cable. We deprecate your opinion that there has been unsportsmanlike play. We have the fullest confidence in captain, team and managers, and are convinced that they would do nothing to infringe either the Laws of Cricket or the spirit of the game. We have no evidence that our confidence has been misplaced. Much as we regret accidents to Woodfull and Oldfield, we understand that in neither case was the bowler to blame. If the Australian Board of Control wish to

Bert Oldfield back home in Killara with wife Ruth and daughters Judith and Ruth Mary.

propose a new law or rule it shall receive our careful consideration in due course. We hope the situation is not now as serious as your cable would seem to indicate, but if it is such as to jeopardise the good relations between English and Australian cricketers, and you consider it desirable to cancel remainder of programme, we would consent with great reluctance'.

The Australian Board of Control's opening salvo was met with a broadside by the uncompromising M.C.C. and was laced with a veiled threat. Not only were two Tests yet to be played but also tour matches against all four Sheffield Shield states, as well as N.S.W. Northern Districts and Combined Country of Queensland. Still in the grip of the Great Depression, these matches would provide a much-needed cash injection to state and regional cricket associations. The four-week break between the Tests created an unfortunate vacuum for recriminations and ill-feeling to percolate. As the England Cricket Team made its way east, the accusation of 'unsportsmanlike' behaviour stuck in their craw, particularly in the case of captain Jardine, who was castled for a single run playing against Ballarat.

In the calm eye of the Bodyline storm, an extraordinary event occurred on the eve of England's second tour match against New South Wales in Sydney. Chronicled in the *Game, Set and Lodge* exhibition at the Library and Museum of Freemasonry, London in 2012 was the invitation by Bert Oldfield to Douglas Jardine, a fellow Freemason, to attend a meeting of his Roseville Lodge on the night of 25 January 1933- only nine days after the Adelaide incident. Evidently the bonds of Masonic brotherhood overwhelmingly trumped the ill-feeling between the Australian and English teams at the time.

Subsiding swelling to his temple and a time of forced reflection left Oldfield in an increasingly obstinate mood, leading to his most steadfast comments regarding the circumstances of his Adelaide injury. In Sydney's *Smith's Weekly* of Saturday 28 January 1933, he quashed reports that he had declared Larwood's ball "a perfectly fair one" in much the same fashion that Woodfull had to deny reports he had apologised to Plum Warner for his Adelaide dressing room comments. "I say definitely...that I gave no such interview", said Oldfield, who was photographed with three strips of sticking plaster fastening a wad of gauze to his forehead. "The ball which struck me on the forehead MAY have been on the wicket-but I am not sure, because I lost sight of it after it left Larwood's hand" he said.

The keeper unleashed his most strident criticism of the Bodyline tactic to date:-

'Body-line bowling...is a menace to cricket and a danger to batsmen...In fairness to Larwood, I could not say that it was pitched in line with my body, because as I say, I lost sight of it. But that refers only to that particular ball. FOR THE WHOLE OF THE TIME I WAS AT THE WICKETS-INDEED, IT HAS BEEN THE SAME IN EVERY MATCH- THERE WAS THAT CONTINUAL POUNDING GOING ON, AND ONLY THOSE WHO HAVE HAD TO FACE IT CAN HAVE ANY IDEA OF ITS SEVERITY.

Body-line bowling is inimical to the best interests of cricket. I have always regarded it as such, and after the Adelaide Test I am more than ever opposed to it'.

Oldfield reserved praise for England fast-bowler Gubby Allen who achieved success while refusing to resort to the Bodyline tactic which he claimed would, "alter the whole character of cricket. It will no longer be a game. Indeed, it is no longer a game now".

On 30 January 1933, the Australian Board of Control sent its reply to the Marylebone Cricket Club:-

'We, Australian Board of Control, appreciate your difficulty in dealing with matter raised in our cable without having seen the actual play. We unanimously regard bodyline bowling as adopted in some of the games in the present tour as being opposed to the spirit of cricket and unnecessarily dangerous to players. We are deeply concerned that the ideals of the game shall be protected, and have therefore appointed a committee to report of the action necessary to eliminate such bowling from all cricket in

Australia as from beginning 1933-34 season. Will forward copy of committee's recommendation for your consideration, and, it is hoped, co-operation, as to its application in all cricket. We do not consider it necessary to cancel remainder of program'.

Striking a more conciliatory tone and invoking the 'spirit of cricket' in contrast to accusations of "unsportsmanlike" conduct, there lingered traces of Jeanes's and Scrymgour's Adelaide shell-shock in the assurances that seeing Bodyline was believing. Ultimately the Board did not call the M.C.C.'s bluff – the tour would continue.

As Oldfield settled into domestic life in Killara, the Australian team for the fourth Test in Brisbane was announced. His replacement was New South Wales back-up gloveman Hammy Love, whom Oldfield had replaced as back-up keeper for the A.I.F. team in 1919. The Australian selectors swung the axe on Jack Fingleton after his pair of ducks in the third Test as well as Clarrie Grimmett following his disappointing 5 wickets at 65.20 over the three Tests. Brought into the squad were Victorians Len Darling and Ernie Bromley and South Australian seamer Bert Tobin. The team looked like a tattered, patched-up outfit and light on bowling options going to the Test that could decide the Ashes.

On 2 February 1933, the M.C.C. replied to the Board of Control with the subtle allusion that the series could still be in jeopardy if the "unsportsmanlike" accusation was not satisfactorily resolved.

'We, the Committee of the Marylebone Cricket Club note with pleasure that you do not consider it necessary to cancel the remainder of programme, and that you are postponing the whole issue involved until after the present tour is completed. May we accept this as clear indication that the good sportsmanship of our team is not in question? We are sure you will appreciate how impossible it would be to play and Test match in the spirit we all

desire unless both sides were satisfied there was no reflection upon their sportsmanship. When your recommendation reaches us it shall receive our most careful consideration and will be submitted to the Imperial Cricket Conference'.

On the eve of the fourth Test the Board of Control relented on its most serious allegation but not its opposition to the Bodyline tactic.

We do not regard the sportsmanship of your team as being in question. Our position was fully considered at the recent meeting in Sydney and is as indicated in our cable of January 30. It is the particular class of bowling referred to therein which we consider is not in the best interests of cricket, and in this view we understand we are supported by many eminent English cricketers. We join heartily with you in hoping that the remaining Tests will be played with the traditional good feeling.

As his beloved team toiled in the Brisbane heat and humidity, Bert and Ruth Oldfield headed to the Blue Mountains outside Sydney, staying at 'The Chalet' in Wentworth Falls. The fresh mountain air revitalised the energetic keeper enough to have him plotting an early return to the game. On 15 February 1933, as Australia was struggling to build a second innings total on Day 5 of the Test match in Brisbane, Oldfield walked onto the Sydney Cricket Ground in his freshly pressed whites. Keeping for the N.S.W. Coaching Team which included future star Bill Brown and New South Wales coaching mentor George Garnsey, Oldfield made 3 stumpings and 49 runs against the Southern Districts Juniors team. Despite it being relative baby steps for a Test cricketer- he was back in the game less than a month after his skull fracture.

That night a solemn vigil was being held in the Queensland capital for young Archie Jackson whose life was fading away in the city's Ingarfield Private Hospital. Midway through the previous year, Jackson had been diagnosed with tuberculosis which had extensively engrossed his lungs. The 23-year-old had moved to Brisbane to be closer to his girlfriend and in the added hope that the warmer weather would help in his recovery. In the evenings during the Test match, both England and Australian players visited him in hospital in his final few days. Out of the playing group and confined in Sydney, Bert Oldfield and Alan Kippax were prevented from paying their final respects. Shortly after midnight on 16 February 1933, Archie Jackson passed away. As dawn broke on Day 6, Australia's hopes of retaining the Ashes had faded with England needing 55 runs to win with 8 wickets in hand. With flags at half-mast in honour of Jackson, the players entered the melancholy arena wearing black armbands to play-out the inevitable result – victory to England and the Ashes lost.

Australian players carry the coffin of Archie Jackson: pallbearers are Victor Richardson, Bill Woodfull, Alan Kippax and Bert Oldfield. Obscured are Bill Ponsford and Don Bradman

The journey to Sydney was a sombre one as both Test teams, Jackson's family and his casket were on the train together. His graveside funeral was conducted at the Field of Mars cemetery in Sydney in front of a vast crowd of mourners. Grief was etched onto the faces of pall-bearers Oldfield, Kippax, Woodfull, Ponsford, Richardson and Bradman as they carried their departed comrade to his final resting place.

Oldfield was afforded a further opportunity to prove himself for the fifth Test in Sydney with games against a visiting Lord Howe Island team. Representing the New South Wales Cricket Association with Jack Fingleton and Tommy Andrews in games at the Sydney Cricket Ground and North Sydney Oval, the keeper performed with no ill-effects. Hammy Love was left to ponder his single Test career as Oldfield was named in the team which included the new faces of South Australian off-spinner Philip 'Perker' Lee and Victorian quick Harry 'Bull' Alexander. Confirming his selection, Oldfield told the *Daily Telegraph* of 18 February 1933, "I feel as fit as ever…I wasn't concerned with myself so much as the possibility of weakening the Test team if I were not at my top again".

England went into the final Test as favourites after seamer Tim Wall withdrew with a foot injury leaving the debutant Alexander as the only genuine pace option. Batting first, the Australians experienced a familiar top-order collapse until Bradman (48), O'Brien (61), McCabe (73) and Darling (85) righted the course of the innings. In a demonstration of sheer imperviousness, Larwood bowled Bodyline against Oldfield with a four-man leg-trap. Despite once again facing the tactic that felled him, the keeper proclaimed his comeback emphatically with one of his four Test half-centuries- scoring 52 in Australia's total of 435. England slightly bested the Australians with 454; Larwood capitalised on his nightwatchman duties until he was dismissed on 98. In a carbon-copy of the Brisbane Test however, the Australians crumpled in the second innings to set England 168 for victory which was achieved on the fifth day before a meagre crowd, for the loss of 2 wickets. Oldfield's consolation was souveniring all three stumps at the striker's end.

The most controversial and bitter series in the history of Test cricket came to an end with England's 4-1 victory and the Ashes regained. The Bodyline tactic, primarily targeting Bradman, had achieved Jardine's aims. Prior to the 1932-33 series, Bradman's Test average was 99.81 but his average for the series was reduced to 56.77 for the four Tests he played. His overall Test average after the series was trimmed to 87.52. The tactic however, had the potential to change the game forever if it was to be adopted around the cricketing world at all levels.

The England Cricket Team was issued a dose of their own medicine when they faced Bodyline tactics from the touring West Indies team in the northern hemisphere summer of 1933. Having witnessed the spectacle, Marylebone Cricket Club legislators deemed the form of bowling 'unfair' and placed enforcement into the hands of the umpires. Having the advantage of witnessing every ball of the Bodyline series so intimately, umpire George Hele said, "only two men, George Borwick and myself, saw from start to finish the five acts of this vicious drama from close quarters and George and I are still unanimous in our views regarding it...if Bodyline had not been banned, there would have been no District, County, or other grade and classes of cricket to watch".

THE KING OF KEEPERS

As the tumultuous 1932-33 cricket season diminished, the irrepressible Oldfield returned to Sydney Grade Cricket to keep wicket for Gordon for the remaining competition games. He also resumed lecturing on cricket with Bodyline still the hot topic; showing his Magigraph footage of the 1930 England tour and the recent Bodyline series and slow-motion studies of himself, Bradman and Grimmett. A *Sydney Morning Herald* journalist was present at one of Oldfield's lectures at the Sydney city Y.M.C.A. and reported in the paper of 28 April 1933 of Oldfield's thoughts regarding Bodyline, "[t]he famous players of the past would not have made a better showing against the methods of the English bowlers, Larwood and Voce, than the present internationals". He responded to criticisms of the Australian captain's conviction not to retaliate with Bodyline tactics saying, "[e]ven if Woodfull did desire to retaliate, he did not have the same forces at his command as Jardine. The tactics could only have been effective when he had fast bowlers, such as the Englishmen". The proceeds of the lecture were donated to the Sudan United Mission charity.

Oldfield paid tribute to Larwood who he claimed had dominated the Australian team, "[d]uring the last Tests, Australia never really had a settled team. That was the fault of Larwood and not the Australian selectors. The series had shown the weaknesses in Australian cricket. There were no conspicuous all-rounders in the team, no medium pace bowlers, while the absence of specialists in the field made the team the weakest in this department for many years. The batting failed repeatedly". He went on to describe Jardine's field-placings as "clever" and continued his public admiration of Woodfull who was "often black and blue from bruises" during the course of the series.

A *Daily Telegraph* reporter present at the same event recorded that Oldfield blamed the poor sightboards at the Adelaide Oval for him losing sight of the Larwood ball. On a subsequent visit to Canberra in May 1933 he was "whistled and cheered by wildly-excited youngsters" when addressing school boys at the city's Capitol Theatre according to the *Canberra Times*. Oldfield urged the boys to reject any attempts to make Bodyline bowling mainstream, saying that cricket was "first and last a sportsman's game" and that it was better to lose a match by fair play than win it by methods of "over-zeal". At an evening session he told adult Canberrans:-

> "The reputation of cricket had already suffered and, if the bodyline attack was to be continued, it would genuinely hinder the progress of the game. That would be a calamity as it stood for such high principles and meant so much to the Empire's prosperity. It was pleasing, therefore, to read the opinions of many past international English players and present day county captains, who all spoke disparagingly of it".

Throughout the months of May and June, the Oldfield caravan wound its way through southern New South Wales and the Riverina entertaining and informing dinner guests and theatre-goers in places like Yass, Goulburn, Wagga Wagga, Gundagai, Tumut, Narrandera, Leeton and Junee. As the extensive tour concluded in northern New South Wales in late-June, public enthusiasm had not abated with the *Tweed Daily* reporting that Oldfield was "mobbed" by boys and girls hunting for autographs in the town of Murwillumbah.

After a couple of months break in Sydney, the veteran keeper made a return to rural New South Wales on a tour which caused a degree of controversy. The New South Wales Cricket Association was accused of commercialising the sport at the expense of rural associations after the Association extended the offer of hosting a team which included superstars Bradman, McCabe, Kippax, Fingleton and Oldfield. The N.S.W.C.A. required a guarantee of £35 (in excess of $3000) from district associations which would also be liable for accommodation, insurance and incidental expenses on top of that amount. The *Dubbo Liberal* of 5 September 1933 reported that the local district association estimated they could be out of pocket by £55 (in excess of $5000) from the visit. In the end, the Dubbo District Cricket Association offered the N.S.W.C.A. £35 to cover all expenses for the entire visit and it went ahead. After other regional bodies initially baulked at the hosting costs, the tour eventuated with civic receptions, dinners and matches held in Mudgee, Dubbo, Cowra, Holbrook, Albury, Leeton and Orange across September. Upon the return to Sydney, with the country still in the grip of the Great Depression, the tourists played in a mid-week charity match to aid the unemployed, held at Chatswood Oval in October. Played between Oldfield and Bradman-captained XIs, Test veterans Kelleway, Macartney and Mailey joined emerging star Bill Brown in a star-studded match.

There would be no Test tour during the 1933-34 Australian cricket summer, so the focus was firmly directed on building a squad for the 1934 Ashes tour of England. The month of October was devoted to grade and district cricket before the commencement of the Sheffield Shield in November, including additional First-Class matches scheduled against minnow states, Tasmania and Western Australia.

Following the First-Class retirement of Hammy Love, Glebe gloveman Frank Easton became Oldfield's New South Wales deputy wicket-keeper. His back-up for the Australian team was emerging as South Australian Charlie Walker who was named in 1934 Ashes tour selection trial matches at the Sydney Cricket Ground. The shape of the tour squad started to materialise with stand-out performances in the Richardson XI versus Woodfull XI and New South Wales versus the Rest of Australia matches. Across the contests, centuries were made by Woodfull, McCabe, Kippax and Fingleton (who would later be unlucky not to be selected) and wickets were taken by accurate fast-medium Victorian Hans Ebeling and Bill O'Reilly. Sheffield Shield performances offered further clarity with Bradman, Bill Brown and a resurgent Alan Kippax dominating with the bat and spinners O'Reilly, Grimmett and 'Chuck' Fleetwood-Smith taking the bulk of the wickets.

By the end of 1933, the smouldering embers left from the raging fires of Bodyline appeared to be contained. In a cable to the Australian Board of Control in December, the Marylebone Cricket Club declared, "[w]e are very glad to know that we may look forward to welcoming the Australians next summer. We shall do all in our power to make the visit enjoyable". The ability of umpires to intervene in what they deemed to be "dangerous" play would become a pivotal consideration in avoiding a repeat of the previous acrimonious Test series.

The traditional Victoria – New South Wales Christmas clash

at Melbourne saw Oldfield away from Ruth and the girls for the festive holiday. Apart from the previous Christmas and the 1924 Ashes Test in Sydney, he had not spent the day with family since returning from the war. Mercifully he was rested for the New Year's home game against Queensland to spend time with his young family which gifted keeping understudy Frank Easton his debut First-Class match.

The customary speculation regarding the composition of the 1934 Ashes touring squad started gaining momentum. Some in the press were advocating for a youth policy, arguing that players like Woodfull and Oldfield have had their time in the spotlight while others were pumping for the inclusion of Bert Ironmonger who would be turning 52 by the time of the first Test. Increasingly viewed as a member of the 'old guard', 39-year-old Oldfield's appointment as replacement captain for Kippax in the late-season match against Victoria was criticised by commentators, including Johnnie Moyes, who favoured giving Bradman a taste of the job.

Either through dissatisfaction with the New South Wales set-up, or his desire for a stable non-cricketing profession – Don Bradman was being lured away from wearing the royal blue cap. Early in 1934, the master batsman was approached by businessman and leading South Australian Cricket Association figure Harry Hodgetts, who offered him a six-year contract to work in his stock and share-broking firm. The move to Adelaide included on-the-job training and time off to play cricket- the decision wasn't an agonising one.

After dinner on the night of 30 January 1934, Australian selectors Bill Woodfull, Dr Charles Dolling and Edmund 'Chappie' Dwyer went into executive session to narrow-down the lucky 16 players. Unsurprisingly, Oldfield was chosen for his fourth Ashes tour to England while Charlie Walker was overlooked as back-up for Victorian keeper Ben Barnett. With a view to the future, Don Bradman was named vice-captain to Woodfull with the team including: McCabe, Kippax, Ponsford, Bromley, Darling, Brown, Grimmett, O'Reilly, Fleetwood-Smith, Wall, Ebeling and a surprise selection being Arthur Chipperfield of Sydney's Western Suburbs club. A poor finish to the 1932-33 Ashes for Fingleton and Richardson outweighed ensuing Sheffield Shield runs in the minds of the selectors who favoured the variety offered by left-handed Victorians Ernie Bromley and Len Darling to break-up the bowler's line.

In the Sydney *Sun* social pages of 1 February 1934, Bert and Ruth Oldfield were pictured drinking tea in the garden at Killara. Dressed in a double-breasted pinstripe suit, Oldfield looked relaxed and satisfied with his recent selection while Ruth, wearing a stylish cloche hat, looked somewhat solemn – possibly at the prospect of being husbandless and looking after two small girls for the next 7 months. The couple attended a farewell ball in Sydney prior to departure where an Australian flag and a golden bag "to hold the [regained] Ashes" was presented to the New South Wales members of the Test team. Before leaving Sydney's Central Station on the Melbourne Express among a throng of well-wishers, Oldfield had a final moment with his young family. Excited by the flashes of press photographers 4-year-old Ruth Mary soaked-up the atmosphere while 2-year-old sister Judith sat pensively in her father's arms, while their parents braved smiles for the cameras.

Departing from Melbourne, the 18th Australian touring team to England played customary matches against Tasmania and Western Australia. The highlight of the sojourn was the performance of Tasmania's Jack Badcock who scored 105 opening against the full Australian Test attack- prompting a move to South Australia to play

The Oldfields: Judith, Bert, Ruth Mary and Ruth in the mid-1930s

Shield cricket and later Test selection. Australia's much-admired captain Bill Woodfull, who still seemed to carry the weight of the Bodyline series on his shoulders, scored twin centuries despite what was becoming an evident declining love for the game.

As the Australians traversed the Indian Ocean on the *Orford*, the voyage was largely uneventful apart from Len Darling suffering a groin strain during a game of deck quoits, which ruled him out of an up-coming tour match in Ceylon. Don Bradman, who was off-colour and underweight, was also sidelined prior to embarkation. During the team's stop-off in Ceylon, the *Evening Standard* of 31 March 1934 reported Douglas Jardine's terse declaration that he had, "neither the intention nor the desire to play cricket against Australia" in the English summer. No doubt the Australian Cricket Team was crushed upon hearing this news.

After arriving in England, Australia commenced the first tour match on 2 May against Worcestershire dashingly with an emphatic win including an innings of 206 from Bradman, 67 from Oldfield and Grimmett's 5 for 53. During the next game in Leicester, Oldfield received a moving off-field surprise when visited by nurses Park and Strange who had treated him for shellshock in Gloucester during the war. The pair admitted that they were too shy to meet him on previous tours but had summoned-up the courage to approach him at the team hotel.

With the first Test due to commence at Trent Bridge, news broke in mid-May that Harold Larwood (still struggling with an injury to his left foot sustained in Australia) was refusing to be made the scapegoat for Bodyline. Not helped by petulant outbursts against Bradman, Woodfull, the Australian Board of Control and Australian crowds in his book *Body-Line?*, the bowler's refusal to sign a letter of apology drafted by administrators meant that his Test career was over. The only fervent Bodyline exponent left standing was Nottinghamshire's Bill Voce who was still available for selection for his country. Taking the opportunity to travel between tour matches, Oldfield went to a bat manufacturer in Nottingham to inspect samples for his business when he ran-into his former adversary, Harold Larwood. The pair was photographed shaking hands in front of a row of bats and piles of curing English willow. With the scar still evident on Oldfield's forehead from the blow sustained 17 months prior, the keeper declared that he bore no grudge – over the ensuing years they would become firm friends.

Despite the loss of Jardine and Larwood, the England Cricket Team looked a strong side, particularly in the batting department.

Herbert Sutcliffe and Walter Hammond were both at the peak of their powers averaging 69.62 and 66.04 respectively after lengthy Test careers.

Woodfull won the toss against stand-in captain Cyril Walters and elected to bat for the first Test of the 1934 Ashes at Trent Bridge in Nottingham. The batting-heavy Australians faced a new-look, but far from intimidating, attack in the form of 40-year-old medium pacer George Geary, Test regular Hedley Verity, debutant pacer Ken Farnes and Bodyline benchwarmer Tommy Mitchell. Most batsmen got starts in the total of 374 with Arthur Chipperfield suffering the ignominy of being the first player to fall for 99 on Test debut. Australia's wrist spin pair of Grimmett

Oldfield back in England demonstrating his stumping prowess

and O'Reilly began their domination of the Test match sharing in 7 dismissals to have England faltering on 268 in reply. Woodfull declared the Australian second innings to set the home side 379 for victory. Oldfield joined-in the fun with two catches and a stumping as O'Reilly (7 for 54) and Grimmett (3 for 39) took all 10 wickets to humble England – all out for 141.

After a short turn-around England hit-back in the second Test at Lord's with a comprehensive victory by an innings and 38 runs to level the series. Centuries to Maurice Leyland (109) and Les Ames (120) and Verity's match figures of 15 for 104 sunk the Australians despite a maiden century from rookie Bill Brown (105).

Oldfield returned once again to his ancestral homeland in Lancashire to play the third Test at Old Trafford in Manchester. In a time-limited four-day Test, the high-scoring affair ended in a draw leaving the series locked at one-apiece heading into the fourth Test in Leeds. While in the North, Oldfield was invited to address Harrogate Girls School by Elizabeth 'Mollie' Child, England women's cricketer and the school's games mistress. Though she was a specialist with the bat, Childs bowled to Oldfield in a batting demonstration. He later gave the students a speech on technical points of the game.

Australia looked to be in the ascension in the fourth Test at Headingley when dismissing England for only 200 runs – Oldfield contributing 2 catches and a pair of stumpings. Sent-in as nightwatchman close to stumps on the first day, Oldfield was caught-behind off a rampant Bill Bowes who had replaced Ken Farnes as spearhead. Bowes then bowled Woodfull to have Australia at 3 for 39 at stumps. If the England Cricket Team felt confident overnight, their hopes were dashed by extraordinary batting performances from Ponsford (181) and Bradman (304) which saw 455 runs amassed on Day 2. Finishing on 584, Australia hoped to dismiss England on the final scheduled day but fell 4 wickets short – the game ending in a draw.

Oldfield was spared having to play in what became the most unpleasant match of the 1934 tour against Nottinghamshire. Antagonised by the absence of Harold Larwood and Arthur Carr, evidently for diplomatic reasons, the Australian team received a cold reception from the parochial locals. Denied a spot in the England bowling attack, Bodyline true believer Bill Voce took his shot at the visitor's batting line-up. Bowling bouncers to a four-man leg-trap, Voce ripped into the Australians dismissing Woodfull, Brown, McCabe, Kippax, Darling, Chipperfield, Barnett and Wall in his 8 for 66 performance off 23 overs.

Prior to the next Australian innings, captain Woodfull approached the executive of the Nottinghamshire County Cricket Club insisting that Voce's tactics breached the conditions on which the tour was organised and advised that the Australian team would not take the field for the rest of the match if it continued. For the remainder of the fixture, Voce was sidelined with "shin soreness" but the crowd saw through it and further directed their ire at the Australians as the match ground-out to a draw. Following an umpire's report to the Nottinghamshire committee, Voce was found guilty of engaging in 'direct attack' bowling.

In a carbon copy of the 1930 Ashes, the deadlocked series came down to a fifth Test decider at The Oval. With luck again on his side, Woodfull won a pivotal coin-toss over counterpart Bob Wyatt and sent his team into bat. Brown's dismissal on 10 brought Bradman to the crease to partner with Bill Ponsford. The pair resumed their Headingley aggression as they slaughtered a hapless England attack including Bowes, Allen, Verity and Hammond. By stumps on the first day, Australia had inflicted a grave psychological blow on the enemy with a 451-run partnership between Bradman (244) and Ponsford (205 not out). After resuming at 2 for 475 on Day 2, Ponsford reached 266 when he was bizarrely dismissed 'hit wicket' in consecutive innings. Australia constructed a commanding total of 701 runs which England could not match despite 110 from Maurice Leyland in the innings of 321. The green caps compounded England's significant deficit to set the home team 707 runs for an unlikely victory. Grimmett (5 for 64), O'Reilly (2 for 58) and McCabe (2 for 5) put the Englishmen to the sword, cutting them down on 145. Australia won the Test by a mammoth 562 runs and regained the cherished Ashes.

As the 1934 tour came to a conclusion in September, a moment of levity ensued for the homesick Australian players. In Margaret Geddes's book *Remembering Bradman,* Bill Brown recalled an amusing incident involving Bert Oldfield and Don Bradman. During the 1920s, British nobleman Sir Henry Dudley Gresham Leveson-Gower began hosting late-season matches on the grounds of his Scarborough residence against touring Test teams. Despite the 14-year age-gap, Brown admits that Oldfield and Bradman's sharp facial features and short stature made them hard to tell apart on occasions. During a dinner for the Leveson-Gower match Brown recollected that the 61-year-old host grabbed Oldfield and said:

"'Come on, dear Don, you must come and dine with me.' And Bert Oldfield being the man he was winked at us and went off and sat down at the top table and this fellow was saying, 'Now Don...' not saying a word to anyone else but devoting his whole time to Don (as he thought he was), and Bert's looking down the table at us and winking. Anyway eventually this fellow was in the middle of a story to Bert and he sees Don sitting down the table with the rest of the team.

He couldn't do anything, he had to go along with it. We're killing ourselves laughing. Don thought it was a great joke".

Bradman would not be laughing for long as matters would take a turn for the worst before he could board the boat home. Seemingly having recovered from his malady at the commencement of the tour, he underwent emergency surgery for acute appendicitis within an hour of admission to hospital. His life in the balance, his wife Jessie Bradman left Adelaide for London fearing the worst.

Across the five Ashes Tests, Oldfield took 8 catches and 6 stumpings but was under-par with the bat scoring 108 runs at an average of 18. Back-up keeper Ben Barnett played more First-Class matches than Oldfield on the tour averaging 33.57 with the bat and taking 18 catches and 12 stumpings in comparison to Oldfield's 22.69 and 21 catches and 19 stumpings. Determined to push-on with his international representative career, the veteran keeper witnessed another era pass in the Australian Cricket Team with the retirements of Ponsford, Kippax, Wall and Woodfull. In no better an example of the selflessness and dignity of Bill Woodfull, and the philosophy that guided his Australian captaincy, he handed a wreath that he was designated to lay at the Anzac memorial in Port Said, Egypt to Oldfield. Disembarked at the port during the homeward leg on 12 October, Woodfull declared that Oldfield was the only "digger" still playing Test cricket therefore it was most appropriate for him to perform the ceremony on behalf of the team.

BOWLING MAIDENS

UPON A VICTORIOUS RETURN to Sydney where he was warmly embraced by wife Ruth and his bonneted daughters, Oldfield was handed the New South Wales captaincy by his long-time teammate and sporting business rival Alan Kippax, who would continue as a player until the season's end. The summer of 1934-35 would not comprise a Test series played by the men, but by the Australian Women's Cricket Team against their English counterparts in the inaugural women's Test series. The three-match event was scheduled for the Brisbane Exhibition Ground, the Sydney Cricket Ground and Melbourne Cricket Ground across December 1934 and January 1935. The rise in women's international cricket had come about in rapid succession to the explosion of popularity with women and girls in the late-1920s resulting in the need for formal organisation and administration.

The New South Wales Women's Cricket Association was formed in Sydney in January 1928. It is believed the first games of female cricket in the state capital began 50 years prior when Lady Murray, the principal of Springfield College, organised matches for girls and young women in a paddock adjacent to the college in Darlinghurst. The first matches under the auspices of the N.S.W.W.C.A. were held on the grounds of Sydney University, Moore Park and the Domain involving teams from the Teachers Training College and City Girls' Amateur Sports Association. By 1929 Sydney University had its own team while the Young Women's Christian Association and the Teacher's Training College fielded two teams each.

Soon after returning from his honeymoon in England, perhaps inspired by his sports-loving wife, Oldfield became involved in the emerging women's cricket movement. A team benefiting from his company's financial sponsorship entered the B grade competition and were known as the 'W.A.Oldfields' – later to become simply-known as the 'Oldfields'. The team's first match was against Lustre Hosiery on 12 October 1929, but the contest was a torrid affair with the Oldfields beaten 36 runs to 27. The Oldfield's captain Evie Carpenter was the best of the bowlers, supported by Peggy Knight and Masie Mudie while Florrie Adair was best with the bat.

Bert Oldfield's monetary support for his eponymous team was not limited to naming sponsorship for advertising purposes as he and business partner Charlie Macartney held coaching sessions for the women on the Domain on Wednesday evenings – which became a Mecca for aspiring female cricketers. Macartney and Oldfield donated two autographed bats to be raffled at the Women's Cricket Sports carnival held at Sydney University on Saturday, 19 October 1929. The skills-based event involved points awarded to competitors across the nine women's teams in disciplines including throwing at the wicket, running between wickets and fielding categories. The Sans Souci team won the carnival with 14 points, beating University by a point.

By November 1929, the Oldfields may have been profiting from the tutelage of their benefactors to the point that it was felt they were becoming too strong for the B-grade competition and on 25 January 1930 they were promoted into the senior grade. Echoing their first game of the season however, the Sydney *Sun* recorded the Oldfield's debut as, "an inauspicious first appearance in a grade match" dismissed for 14 runs in reply to the Cypress team's 92. While many of the matches were low-scoring affairs, player's skills continued to improve during the competition and team scores increasingly passed triple-figures including San Souci's 3 for 108 which included 41 from future Test all-rounder, Essie Shevill.

A national body to administer women's cricket was first discussed at a meeting of the N.S.W.W.C.A. in early 1930 which would bring together similar state bodies in varying stages of organisation in Victoria, Queensland and South Australia. By April that year the first interstate women's matches since the First World War were held between Victoria and two New South Wales teams at the Sydney Cricket Ground number 2 across the Easter long-weekend. Oldfields batting mainstay, Masie Mudie, was selected for the Essie Shevill-captained New South Wales Second XI team.

On Saturday 19 April 1930, a two-innings match commenced after an official lunch at the Centennial Park kiosk between the New South Wales Second XI and Victoria. The southern tourists were victorious by six wickets and later attended an event with the other teams at the State Theatre in the city.

A well-patronised New South Wales First XI match against Victoria on the Monday sparked additional interest from the adjacent arena with the *Sydney Morning Herald* of the following day reporting that, "[a] large number of spectators watched the game which proved more attractive to hundreds on the embankment at the Sports Ground than the football [a rugby league match between Balmain and Newcastle] they had gone to see". Many attendees of the Royal Easter Show, being held at nearby showgrounds, reportedly filed-in to watch the local side beat the visitors by 53 runs.

The carnival became a prelude to the proposed formation of an All-Australian Women's Cricket Council. The ambitious plan for women's cricket involved yearly carnivals between the four Sheffield Shield states and hosting tours from English and New Zealand touring teams. In May 1930, secretary of the N.S.W.W.C.A, Margaret Peden, had sent a temporary constitution for the council to her Queensland and Victorian counterparts with a view to holding a national carnival in March 1931. By the end of the year, the associations of New South Wales, Victoria and Queensland became the foundation members of the national governing body for women's cricket in Australia with South Australia applying for affiliation a year later. The triangular carnival was contested between the three states on the Sydney Cricket Ground No.2 and the grounds of the Cranbrook school in Sydney's Rose Bay. While New South Wales and the Victorians eventually tied on 1 win each, the home-side won the tournament on average per wicket.

By the end of 1930, the women's cricket craze which was sweeping Australia took a turn towards the fanatical after a bizarre incident in Newcastle on Sunday 2 November which was chronicled in the *Newcastle Sun* of the following Friday:-

'The Town Clerk (Mr. Glassop) said that it had been reported to him that the women cricketers upset a male cricket game on Birdwood Park, and took possession of it for themselves.

Annoyed because the men were on the wicket, the women, the report alleges, tore up the stumps, flung the bails about, and tried to rip the matting from the pitch. It grew hot for the men, and they left'.

The women cricketers were also accused of using "very unparliamentary language" during their disruption of the men's match. Despite "indignant denials" from the accused women cricketers and counter allegations that it was the men's fault, the Mayor of Newcastle decreed that sporting activities were to be banned at Birdwood Park on Sundays for both women and men. The prohibition would later be overturned once tempers had cooled.

Competition for playing space came under the spotlight once again with comments from a local councilman in Victoria making news nationally. An application by women's cricketers to access a local reserve was addressed at a meeting of the Collingwood local council on Tuesday 9 February 1932. Councillor Marshall made the following disparaging remarks:-

> "These women now want to start depriving the children of their playground. I think it would be better if no Australian girls played cricket. Anyhow, with the tennis next door, it is nothing but a leg show. It would be better to have a decent men's match there, instead of having a lot of girls playing 'nanny'".

When approached for comment, South Australian Women's Cricket Association secretary, Mrs R. Miller, retorted:

> "What a nerve...[a] nice type of girl has taken up cricket. They are most particular about their costumes and conduct. People seem to be getting a wrong impression about girls playing cricket".

The application was granted in spite of the councillor's fervent objection.

Shortly before the inaugural women's Test cricket series in 1934-35 (which England won 2-0), Oldfield lent his name to a second team, providing sponsorship for a new side in the Newcastle women's competition. His financial support of the 'W.A.Oldfields' teams continued until the outbreak of the Second

World War after which teams were named by district affiliation in preference to commercial sponsorship. While the credit for the emergence of women's cricket in Australia in the 1920s and 1930s goes overwhelmingly to the women players and administrators, Bert Oldfield was arguably the most high-profile cricketing identity to champion the women's game through his financial, technical and moral support.

THE ACCIDENTAL CAPTAIN

OLDFIELD HAD BARELY RECOVERED his land-legs after stepping off the *Orontes* in November 1934 before assuming the role of full-time New South Wales Cricket Team captain in unexpected circumstances. Upon standing down from the position, Alan Kippax anointed Stan McCabe as his replacement. Batting in the Woodfull-Ponsford testimonial match in Melbourne however, McCabe was struck on the hand necessitating him to retire hurt on 5. He would only participate in one match for the rest of the season, leaving Oldfield the natural choice to take the captaincy reins.

According to Oldfield confidant Charlie Macartney, while capable, he had no particular ambition to be a captain, contending, "[he] does not hanker after the position, as he has quite enough to keep him employed during the progress of the match in guarding the stumps and keeping his eye on every single ball bowled".

In the first match of the 1934/35 Sheffield Shield against South Australia at the Sydney Cricket Ground, Oldfield led his young side by example scoring 88 and taking two catches and a pair of stumpings in the victory. In the return match in Adelaide, the S.A.C.A.s were missing the services of their star signing, with Bradman only just leaving from England in December following his emergency appendectomy and ensuing peritonitis. Oldfield notched-up his second victory as captain of the royal blues with a stumping and two catches.

Away once again from Ruth and the girls for Christmas, Oldfield and the New South Welshmen were not shown festive hospitality by their Victorian hosts. A new-look team, following the retirement of Woodfull and Ponsford, made a commanding total of 558 with centuries from O'Brien, Rigg, Darling and Bromley. Left-arm wrist spinner 'Chuck' Fleetwood-Smith caned the visitors with match figures of 11 for 228 – handing Victoria the win. It would be a breakout season for the tall Victorian 'Chinaman' topping the Shield with 60 wickets at an average of 18.95, including eight 5-fors and three 10-fors. With Fleetwood-Smith's selection for Test honours looking increasingly likely, it would be vital for the ageing Oldfield to master keeping to the rare style of bowling for the time, with its peculiarities and variations.

Oldfield sat atop the dismissals list for the 1934-35 season with 13 catches and 12 stumpings ahead of his Victorian rival Ben Barnett, with 13 and 4 respectively. The youthful Victorian team led by Hans Ebeling won the Sheffield Shield with five victories in their six matches largely on the back of Fleetwood-Smith's performances, while Oldfield's first full season of captaincy yielded a middling three wins and three losses.

Off the field, Oldfield became only the third life member of the Victorian branch of the Returned Services League as the guest of honour at an event held at Anzac House in Melbourne during the Woodfull-Ponsford testimonial match. His A.I.F. teammates Allie Lampard, Cyril Docker and Hammy Love were in attendance while letters in praise of Oldfield from Nip Pellew and Jack Gregory were read to the audience. Upon returning to Sydney, he signed with the Australian Broadcasting Commission to provide commentary and expert analysis of the Sheffield Shield season in quarter-hour segments broadcast nightly at 9pm.

In the *Smith's Weekly* of 9 February 1935, Oldfield penned an article in which he left no doubt about his monarchist leanings, declaring his great admiration for British sovereign King George V. "Of all the great honors [sic] that it has been my privilege to receive, I consider by far the greatest to be my meeting with King George" said Oldfield. He outlined times he had seen the King from afar during his time with the A.I.F. in England and the many opportunities playing in the Australian team had afforded him to get to know the King personally through visits to Windsor and Sandringham castles.

"He showed to me, by virtue of his conversation, that his interest in cricket and all Empire sport, as well as his interest in Australia, was very real and not fictitious. His remarks when meeting any of us were conclusive evidence of this.

Again in 1934, His Majesty took personal interest in all our Test matches and when he was out of London he had the latest information regarding the games relayed to him hourly".

It was speculated that after so many meetings with the monarch that Oldfield was the Australian who had shaken the king's hand the most times.

In what would become commonplace for top-line cricketers many decades later, Oldfield took the unusual step of taking his family on tour. Bert, Ruth and the girls travelled to Perth on a steamer to coincide with two end-of-season games against Western Australia at the W.A.C.A. ground in March 1935. Oldfield captained both 3-day matches for New South Wales which ended in draws. Such non-Sheffield Shield First-Class matches by state or combined teams, coupled with tour matches from Test teams, were vital in developing cricket in the West prior to the state's admission to the national competition in the 1947/48 season.

The retirement of Bill Woodfull from Test and First-Class cricket lead to speculation regarding his replacement as Australian captain with a tour of South Africa scheduled to commence in October 1935. In the press, Oldfield was being touted as the front-runner for future captain with Hans Ebeling coming-in second after his breakout success with Victoria. Doubt was cast as to whether Victor Richardson would be considered as he failed to make selection for the 1934 Ashes and looked likely to lose the South Australian captaincy to Don Bradman, who himself was doubtful to tour following his illness and work commitments.

In April, the touring team for South Africa was announced:-
Barnett
Brown
Chipperfield
Darling
Fingleton
Fleetwood-Smith
Grimmett
McCabe
McCormick
O'Brien
Oldfield
O'Reilly
Richardson
Seivers
Forty-one year-old Richardson scraped into the team, more the

beneficiary of seniority and experience than outstanding batting form. Unusually the publication of the team was not accompanied by the announcement of captain and deputy positions. It may have been due to the lingering doubts that Oldfield, despite being named in the squad, was having about going on the South African tour. When pressed by the *Referee* newspaper on 9 May 1935, his reply was, "[i]t is a matter I cannot determine at this stage…It differs from a tour in England. There you leave Australia at the end of summer and are absent in winter. On this tour one has to be absent during the whole of summer. As you will see, it is a business problem into which sentiment cannot obtrude too much. And-there are other considerations". His cryptic clue about "other considerations" may be explained in Ruth accompanying him for the first time on his annual winter speaking tour which wound down the Hume Highway taking-in towns like Echuca and Moama all the way to Melbourne – the life of a semi-professional cricketer with a young family was possibly taking its toll.

Compounding Oldfield's concerns about being away from home so regularly was a disturbing incident which again had him engaging the services of the New South Wales constabulary. On 29 March 1935, he had returned home to his Killara residence to find that it had been ransacked and an estimated £102 ($10,000) worth of items, including clothing, stolen. The police investigation led to a 34-year-old clerk by the name of Leslie Arthur James charged with house breaking and stealing and committed to stand trial. Appearing before the Sydney Quarter Sessions Court in July, it was disturbingly revealed that James committed the offence with a loaded pistol. When asked why he had a loaded weapon in his possession by Judge Curlewis, James replied, "I was disgusted with myself and was thinking of committing suicide". The Judge said he did not accept James's explanation, having

heard it previously from another accused, and believed the red herring was doing the rounds of the criminal fraternity when caught committing offences whilst armed. To set an example of James, Judge Curlewis sentenced him to 2-years imprisonment and declared him a habitual criminal. Only £40 ($4000) of the stolen property was recovered.

Acknowledging her status as Australia's senior 'cricket widow', Ruth Oldfield was approached for comment by the *Daily Telegraph* in light of a controversy arising from the South African Cricket Team's 1935 tour of England. Under touring rules, the wives of Springbok players Jock Cameron and Jack Siedle were forced to stay in separate hotels to their husbands and were only allowed to communicate with them during breaks in play. Ruth told the reporter, "I have not been through that experience…but I can understand how they must feel". She admitted she no longer got nervous watching her husband play:

> "Bert has been playing too long for that…[o]f course I am proud of him and I'll admit that when he does something marvellous I forget myself a little. But I am more delighted when he gets some runs than when he does something well in his place as wicketkeeper. I always urge Bert to get runs, and whenever I am looking on he tries harder. My home duties make it impossible for me to see every match in which Bert plays, but I go when I have the opportunity. The broadcasting of Test matches has done a lot to bring me closer to him when he has been on the other side of the world".

SAVIOUR OF LIONS

On 23 July 1935, Oldfield confirmed in the press that he had formally accepted an invitation to tour South Africa in the coming summer with the Australian team. Confessing that he was close to declining due to business and family reasons, he decided his experience was needed in the young team to maintain the prestige of Australian cricket abroad, following the retirements of major players and Don Bradman being unavailable. Shortly before the team's departure for South Africa captaincy speculation was finally laid to rest with Victor Richardson handed the top job and Oldfield controversially overlooked as vice-captain for Stan McCabe. Australian Board of Control chairman Aubrey Oxlade defended the Board's decision to not appoint the New South Wales captain to the deputy position as they were looking to the future by giving a younger player leadership experience. Oxlade paid tribute to Oldfield's contribution to the Australian Cricket Team over the years and said he would be free to concentrate fully on his wicket-keeping duties which were vital to the team's success.

Keen photographers Bert Oldfield, Clarrie Grimmett and Bill O'Reilly stood on the forecastle of the *Ulysses* snapping away upon entering Durban harbour on 14 November 1935, where they were later greeted by an enthusiastic gathering of locals at a civic reception. Joy was tempered however by the recent news that South African wicket-keeper Jock Cameron had died of enteric fever at the age of 30, shortly after arriving home from the tour of England. The transitional Australian team was the first to tour South Africa in 14-years, Oldfield being the only player who had last toured in 1921. The five-month schedule included 14 matches and a series of Tests – the first five-match series played by Australia on South African soil since Clem Hill's side of 1910-11.

Back home, Ruth Oldfield did not allow loneliness to take hold, organising tennis parties on the backyard court of 'Poitiers'. Frequent visitors were her sisters, Jean and Risse Hunter who would cross the Sydney Harbour Bridge from Randwick in their sandy-coloured Packard to play with nieces, Ruth and Judith.

Oldfield's services were barely needed in the first Test at Kingsmead, Durban with the Australian bowling attack hitting the pegs of the Springboks on 12 occasions across two innings. Australia won by 9 wickets with century contributions from McCabe (149) and Chipperfield (109) while Oldfield got a duck and a lone stumping.

The home side mounted a comeback in the second Test at the Old Wanderers Ground in Johannesburg over Christmas 1935. Dismissed cheaply for 157 and in arrears of the Australians by 93 runs going into their second innings, the South Africans took the lead through a commanding total of 491 thanks largely to Dudley Nourse's mammoth 231. Set an unlikely 398 runs for victory, the Australians held-out for a draw with the match and innings ending on 2 for 274 – Stan McCabe 189 not out. Oldfield made 44 and took a pair of stumpings and 2 caught-behinds.

A tour of South Africa and Rhodesia (modern day Zimbabwe) offered the Australian cricketers myriad opportunities to experience the uniqueness of the African continent. The tourists visited the Vaal River diamond diggings in the Kimberley, went down the East Godault gold mine, donned wet-weather gear for a close-up view of Victoria Falls and admired the wildlife of the Kruger National Park. Oldfield was particularly taken with the majestic lions of South Africa and made an extraordinary intervention for one creature on 'death row'. In the city of East London for the tour match against Border in January 1936, he had heard news of a privately-owned lion in Bloemfontein whose owner had died, with no-one willing to take ownership of the animal – it was scheduled to be destroyed. Oldfield made telephone inquiries and successfully intervened half-an-hour before the lion was slated to be shot. Making the most of connections back in Australia, the keeper made arrangements for the spared creature to be shipped to Sydney where the Taronga Park Zoo gladly provided an enclosure for the fortunate creature.

Twin centuries from openers Bill Brown (121) and Jack Fingleton (112) saw Australia off to a great start in the rain-affected third Test at Newlands in Cape Town. Declaring on 8 for 362, the Australians dismissed the Springboks for 102 and 182 – Clarrie Grimmett the destroyer with 10 wickets for the match.

At 41-years of age, Oldfield scored one of his six First-Class centuries, top-scoring with 132 in Australia's victory against Griqualand West in the New Year tour match at the Athletic

Club Ground in Kimberley. In a big partnership with opener Leo O'Brien (113), Oldfield was the dominant partner hitting fourteen 4s and two 6s. Following the innings the keeper expressed his concern at the news of King George V's failing health as it swept across the British Empire. Oldfield recalled the King's "lovable, fatherly interest in visitors" from his many encounters with the monarch. King George V would later die on 20 January 1936.

Oldfield found himself in the rare position of taking to the field barehanded, in the tour match against Transvaal in Johannesburg prior to the fourth Test. Confined to 12th man duties, an injury to Leo O'Brien required him to substitute while his deputy Ben Barnett held court behind the stumps. In the Test, Grimmett bagged another 10-wicket haul, which included two Oldfield stumpings. Set 157 by South Africa, Australia led by Fingleton (108) scored 439. The pace of McCormick (3 for 28) and the wily turn of Grimmett (7 for 40) dismantled the demoralised opposition for 98 runs which handed Australia an unassailable 3-0 series win.

Back in Durban for the final Test, Australia won its third match in a row by more than an innings. Coincidentally, Fingleton scored his third century in a row (118) and Grimmett his third 10-wicket performance in as many tests (7 for 100 and 6 for 73).

The undefeated Australians had been so dominating that concerns were raised over a scheduled benefit match for Jock Cameron's widow against Transvaal in Johannesburg. Doubts were cast that the cricketing public would turn-out in numbers to witness another flogging which would in-turn affect the amount of funds raised. The novel proposal that the event be a game of baseball gained momentum. Australian cricketers were not strangers to the American game with many early- 20th century notables like Jack Ryder, Bill Ponsford and Alan Kippax playing the sport during the wintertime. The touring squad to South

Africa had a fair share of baseball talent with Len Darling and Ernie McCormick representing Victoria and Victor Richardson playing for South Australia. Bill Brown and Leo O'Brien had also played for club teams in their respective cities.

Three-thousand spectators turned-out for the game on 7 March 1935 for the benefit of the H.B.Cameron Memorial Fund. The Australians wore uniforms donated by the Wanderers Baseball Club while they wore their own Baggy Green caps and cricket boots. Oldfield stayed on the bench in favour of Victor Richardson who had been catcher for the South Australian team in the early-20s while Leo O'Brien took the mound as pitcher. The infield consisted of McCormick (first base), Barnett (second base), Fingleton (short stop) and Darling (third base) with McCabe, Brown and Grimmett in the outfield. Old habits 'died hard' for Clarrie Grimmett discarding his glove and taking the winning catch barehanded to defeat the Transvaal team 12-5 in the ninth inning.

The Australian Cricket Team lining-up to play baseball at the Old Wanderers ground in Johannesburg. While dressed for the occasion, Bert Oldfield (far right) sat the game out on the sidelines.

Many players considered the 1935-36 tour of South Africa the happiest of their careers with much credit going to captain Victor Richardson who fostered a strong team spirit and brought the best out of the men in his charge. The tour also formed a strong bond between the growing number of Irish-Catholic members of the team including O'Reilly, McCabe, Fingleton, O'Brien, McCormick and Fleetwood-Smith.

After 15 years in the Australian Test team, and entering middle-age, Oldfield was still maintaining a solid level of fitness and consistency despite lingering concerns he was struggling to pick Chuck Fleetwood-Smith's wrong-un. Behind the stumps he snared 9 catches and 14 stumpings in the South Africa series. His batting average for the Tests was 24.20 with a high of 44 while his tour average was 34.30 thanks largely to his innings of 132. He also participated in the second-highest partnership (219 runs) of the tour with Victorian Leo O'Brien against Griqualand West. *Referee* cricket journalist J.C. Davis, writing under the pseudonym 'Not Out', wrote of Oldfield in a series review on 2 April 1936: "[h]is efficiency as batsman allied with super-excellence as wicket-keeper, has made Oldfield a great public favourite, because, with it he combines grace in keeping wickets and a high-prized quality in batsmanship that is always seen best under the inspiration of a fight".

Back in Australia, many in cricketing circles were pondering whether the South African series would be Oldfield's last, including former Australian captain Monty Noble who nominated promising Queensland keeper Don Tallon as his possible successor. When cabled by the *Daily Telegraph*, the veteran sent the following reply from Cape Town: "You can deny any report that I intend to retire from First-Class cricket on my return. I love the game and its influences, and I have no wish at the moment to retire – OLDFIELD". The issue was settled.

PETER PAN OF CRICKETERS

OF THE PLAUDITS THAT welcomed Oldfield upon his return to Sydney, none could eclipse the tribute bestowed on him by 75-year-old former Test cricketer Jack Worrall, who debuted for Australia in 1885, coined the term 'body-line' and was still writing on the game. In an article which declared Oldfield as the "Peter Pan of Cricketers", Worrall said his achievements as Australia's wicket-keeper had equalled, if not exceeded that of his former teammate, Jack Blackham- widely considered to be the nation's greatest gloveman. Worrall said in the *Daily Telegraph* of 17 April 1936, " [m]uch as I think of old Jack Blackham...I can hardly say that he was better than Oldfield. In many respects the two stumpers were equally proficient. For example, if a wonderful thing had to be done in a match, such as an extraordinary stumping on the leg-side or a superb catch, Blackham would bring it off; so would Oldfield".

Wearing matching berets and sailor-style outfits, daughters Ruth (5) and Judith (3) proudly watched their father in the 1936 Anzac Day march. Oldfield had a light schedule of promotional speaking engagements during the winter, where in addition to cricket, he projected home movies of his recent South African safari to audiences in Bathurst and Dubbo.

On 11 June 1936, Australian selector Dr Charles Dolling, who had initially treated Oldfield's head injury during the 1933 Adelaide Test, died suddenly of a seizure at the age of 49. Don Bradman immediately filled Dolling's vacancy on the selection panel which would be considering the team for the up-coming Ashes series in the summer of 1936-37. A decision on the appointment of the captain and vice-captain of that side would be a determination of the Board of Control.

A testimonial match for Oldfield's former A.I.F., New South Wales and Australian teammates Warren Bardsley and Jack Gregory, held in Sydney, doubled as an Ashes trial match with teams captained by incumbent Test skipper Victor Richardson and his younger rival Don Bradman. Oldfield played in the Richardson XI which was largely made-up of recent South African tourists while the Bradman team had a youthful, underdog-feel. Batting first, the Richardson XI scored 363 with a century from Bill Brown (111); Oldfield second top-scored with 78. The surprise package for Bradman's XI was the performance of South Australian leg-spinner Frank Ward with 7 for 127 off 32 overs.

Watched by 19,858 spectators on the second day, Bradman played a dominant innings in reply, particularly targeting Bill O'Reilly's bowling, with 212 out of a total of 385 supported by Leo O'Brien (85) and Alan McGilvray (42). The Bradman XI's second-string attack lead again by Ward (5 for 100), humbled the Richardson XI – dismissing them for 180. The lesser-fancied Bradman-led team won the match by 6 wickets over the Richardson XI with the sting in the tail being Richardson's personal failure of 26 and 0. The balance of power in the Australian Cricket Team on-and-off the field began tilting ever-so-slightly. Shifting sands in state ranks saw Oldfield relinquishing his New South Wales captaincy to Stan McCabe following his appointment to the Australian vice-captaincy in the previous Test series. Broadcaster and journalist Alan McGilvray was appointed McCabe's deputy and would perform the role for the bulk of the season with the new captain's Ashes commitments.

England's 1936-37 Ashes touring team had a blend of youth and experience. Hammond, Leyland, Ames, Verity and Voce had all toured previously with players including Arthur Fagg, Charlie Barnett, Ken Farnes and Joe Hardstaff Jr making their first expedition to the hot, dry continent. Australian-born Gubby Allen was appointed captain of the team with a more gracious, diplomatic approach to the game than his predecessor, Douglas Jardine.

Freed of tactical duties, Oldfield was busy behind the stumps for the New South Wales tour match against England in Sydney. Despite fluffing a Walter Hammond inside-edge off a Bill O'Reilly googly, he stumped the dangerous master batsman in both innings – taking his match tally to three. The fixture saw the emergence of yet another Australian leg-spinner in the form of Harold Mudge who took 6 for 42 and 2 for 86 in the New South Wales victory.

At the time New South Wales was playing England in Sydney, the incumbent Australian Test 42-year-old captain Victor Richardson was playing under the leadership of 28-year-old Don Bradman for South Australia against Victoria in Melbourne. While Richardson was in South Africa the previous summer with the Test team, Bradman had led South Australia undefeated through the season to the state's first Sheffield Shield win in nine years. The captaincy role appeared to agree with Bradman with personal figures of 739 runs at an average of 123.16 and a high score of 357. A hint of the Board of Control's future intentions was Bradman's nomination as captain of the Australian XI team in the tour match against the M.C.G..

As the Australian team announcement approached, Oldfield

had the backing of Woodfull, Kippax, Noble and former Australian wicket-keeper J.J. Kelly, who opined in the *Sun* of 22 November that, "[i]t would be a serious matter for us if Oldfield were dropped for the first Test. The side would be a little at sea if a change were made at such a late hour".

The team announced for the first Test was the following:
Badcock
Bradman
Brown
Chipperfield
Fingleton
McCabe
McCormick
Oldfield
O'Reilly
Robinson
Sievers
Ward.

With Queensland's Don Tallon and Victoria's Ben Barnett snapping at his heels, Oldfield made the cut in defiance of the creeping youth policy. Despite wanting to play-on, Victor Richardson and Clarrie Grimmett found themselves dumped from Australia's Test ranks – the latter after the extraordinary performance of 10-wicket hauls in each of his last three Tests. Days later came the official confirmation that Bradman would be the Australian Test captain with McCabe as his deputy.

In the lead-up to the 1936-37 Ashes, the Board of Control set its allowances for Test players and umpires. Players were paid £30 ($2938) for each timeless Test match with a 25s-a-day ($122) incidentals allowance. For interstate players, the Board covered the fare for a first-class sleeping car; players were required to arrive a clear day before the match. Test umpires living in the city of play were paid £10 ($976) while interstate umpires received £15 ($1464). In the mid-1930s, Sheffield Shield players were paid a flat rate of 17s 6d-a-day ($84) and were not reimbursed for lost salary from their normal jobs. As the average annual salary at the time was around £370 ($36,123) it is clear that cricket was only a part-time job for First-Class cricketers and elucidates why some walked away from the game early due to financial considerations.

Disaster seemed to plague the new-look Australian Cricket Team on the eve of the first Test at the Gabba in Brisbane. The Board of Control's requirement of players making their own accommodation arrangements came into focus when some struggled to find lodgings in the city after getting off the train. Jack Fingleton and Ray Robinson were able to land a double room in a hotel overlooking a noisy rail-line. Robinson quipped that it looked likely they would have to find a "decent place in the park". Robinson made his debut with three others: Morris Seivers, Frank Ward and Tasmanian-born Jack Badcock who replaced Bill Brown after he suffered a broken thumb.

Winning the toss, Gubby Allen elected to bat but he may have regretted the decision with opener Stan Worthington top-edging to Oldfield off McCormick's first ball of the Test. Arthur Fagg (4) was also caught-behind and Wally Hammond became McCormick's third victim with the score on 3 for 20. Charlie Barnett (69) and Maurice Leyland (126) consolidated to take England's first innings to 358. Justification for 42-year-old Oldfield's selection was beyond question with critics agreeing that his keeping performance was as good as ever – including 3 catches.

Australia's long-running vulnerability to fast bowling was exposed in their first innings on the lively Gabba wicket exploited by a rampant Bill Voce (6 for 41) and Gubby Allen (3 for 71).

Apart from Fingleton (100) scoring his record fourth century in successive Test innings, only Bradman (38) and McCabe (51) passed double-figures in the innings of 234.

For the England second innings, Australia was without the services of fast bowler McCormick, who frustratingly pulled-out with lower back pain while initially looking in dangerous form. After snaring three stumpings, Oldfield was 'in the wars' after Allen padded a ball away off Ward which deflected into the keeper's left eye. Oldfield left the field with blood gushing from the wound escorted by both captains, but returned soon after being patched-up with sticking plaster.

England set the locals 381 runs for victory, but Brisbane weather conspired against Bradman and his team with rain creating a 'sticky' wicket on the final day. After the loss of Fingleton and Badcock for a pair of ducks, Bradman manipulated the batting order in the hope the wicket would dry-out in time for a recovery mission. Chipperfield (36 not out) and Oldfield (10) were the only batsmen to show any resistance to the onslaught as Allen (5 for 36) and Voce (4 for 16) tore through the Australians who collapsed on 58, losing the first Test by 322 runs. Adding injury to insult, leg-spinner Frank Ward suffered a broken nose in his innings of 1.

Oldfield's wicket-keeping performance was arguably the highlight of the first Test for Australia. He drew level to former England keeper Dick Lilley's record of 84 dismissals in Ashes Tests. In 33 Tests against England, Oldfield had taken 54 catches and 30 stumpings in comparison to Jack Blackham's 36 and 24 in 35 Tests and Sammy Carter's 35 and 17 in 21 matches.

Such was the admiration for Oldfield that N.S.W. South Coast poet Gordon Stanton expressed the country's sentiments for the Australian wicket-keeper in verse:-

You have caught the public fancy
By your skill behind the stumps
You're an energetic chappy
With a manner neat and snappy
And we know you're always happy
Where the ball swings in or bumps.

You're at home to any bowling
Ah, this fact you've often proved
Be they medium, slow or faster
You can take them like a master
Just a slip – and then disaster
For the bails are quickly removed.

You're the acme of perfection
You're the backbone of our side
You're the wicket keeping wonder
For you seldom blunder
And though even we go under
We will look on you with pride.

The Australian team's poor run of luck continued in the second Test in Sydney prior to Christmas 1936. Batting first after winning the toss again, England reached 6 declared for 426 with a masterly 231 by Walter Hammond batting on his happy hunting ground. The Australian batting order was annihilated again on a wet wicket making a paltry 80 runs. The only highlight for the Sydney crowd was a rare swashbuckling innings from Bill O'Reilly, who hit three 6s and two 4s in his top-score of 37. Putting-up a better fight in the second innings, McCabe (93), Bradman (82) and Fingleton (73) helped get the total to a more respectable 324, but lost by an innings and 22 runs. With a pair of singles to his name, the *Sydney Morning Herald* opined that, "[i]t is unfortunate that the batting form of Oldfield has been unsound, but Oldfield's wicket-keeping has been so good that the selectors are not likely to drop him at this stage in favour of a wicketkeeper whom they might consider is a better bat".

After a pair of thumping losses, Bradman's nightmare introduction to Test captaincy and his personal performances of 38, 0, 0 and 82 led to rumours of poor morale in the Australian camp. Under the explosive headline 'Bradman Not Fully Supported by Team', the *Daily Telegraph* of 23 December 1936 reported that the Board of Control and selectors (including Bradman) were "disturbed by a suggestion" that the team was not "pulling together" under Bradman.

"There has definitely, and has for some time, an important section of the team that has not seen eye to eye with Bradman, either on or off the field. In the circumstances Bradman's captaincy has been seriously handicapped".

A clue to the clique undermining Bradman's captaincy was hinted at by the *Telegraph* writer, and it had its origins in the previous Test tour:-

"In cricket circles it has been suggested that Victor Richardson should be called back to heal a breach that does not go deeply, and to co-ordinate the team into the combination it showed in South Africa".

On Christmas Eve, unnamed Board of Control officials described the reports as "bunkum" and Bradman was forced to deny the rumours publicly saying that he had the support of his team and that it was, "unfortunate that a rumor [sic] such as this should be spread at a time when the Australian eleven has suffered successive defeats. More good would accrue if the

Englishmen were given credit for their well-deserved victories". Vice-captain Stan McCabe followed with his own statement: "Don has made a good fist of the captaincy. We are right behind him, and we are a happy family. We are all determined to do better".

Mired in controversy, the third Test of the 1936-37 Ashes commenced on New Year's Day at the Melbourne Cricket Ground. Despite the 2-0 deficit, Melburnians packed their sacred ground in droves, perhaps due to the novelty of the huge new 30,000-seater southern grandstand. Chuck Fleetwood-Smith was a welcome inclusion to the team after recovering from an injury on the South African tour. He was joined by Bill Brown, Len Darling and Keith Rigg who replaced Chipperfield, O'Brien, the injured McCormick and the unwell Badcock.

The Ashes looked to be all but lost on the first day as Australia slumped to 6 for 130 after Bradman won his first toss of the series. McCabe and Oldfield joined forces to hold-on until stumps to take the total to 181. A wet Australian summer now turned on the England team with a heavy overnight shower prompting Bradman to declare early on Day 2 to target his opponents on a 'sticky' wicket. Tall, fast-medium bowler Morris Sievers (5 for 21) justified his continued selection combining with equally-lofty Bill O'Reilly (3 for 28) to erode the English innings which Allen declared on 9 for 76 – hoping to drag the Australians into a deathroll in the same quagmire.

Echoing his first Test strategy, Bradman reversed the batting order in the hope of protecting the batsmen as the pitch stabilised. The unlikely opening batting pairing of Bill O'Reilly and Chuck-Fleetwood Smith did not last long at the crease with O'Reilly out caught-and-bowled by Voce off the first ball. The in-coming batsman Frank Ward, more accustomed to the number 10 position, held-on with his partner until stumps.

A record crowd of 87,798 crammed into the 'G' on the third day as the hot, unimpeded sun baked the Merri Creek soil out in the centre. At the fall of Keith Rigg's wicket with the score on 5 for 97, Jack Fingleton and Don Bradman formed an unlikely middle-order partnership coming-in at 6 and 7 respectively. The packed ground witnessed a record sixth-wicket partnership of 346 unfold with Fingleton scoring 136 and Bradman 270 – the then highest score by an Australian Test captain on home soil. Set 688 runs for victory, England reached 323 on the back of a Maurice Leyland century (111) but fell victim to Fleetwood-Smith (5 for 124) and O'Reilly's (3 for 65) wrist spin. At this point, it was observed by the cricketing press that Oldfield had overcome any doubts regarding his keeping to Fleetwood-Smith.

A masterly captain's knock and pivotal tactical decisions from Bradman contributed to the team's reversal of fortunes in a must-win Test match. The victory, on top of a record aggregate attendance of 350,534 and monumental gate-taking, would presumably have affirmed the new captain's position and the health of team morale amongst players and administrators alike. In an inexplicably poorly-timed manoeuvre, the Board of Control summoned O'Reilly, McCabe, O'Brien and Fleetwood-Smith from the post-match dressing-room into the Victorian Cricket Association offices (the notable absence being journalist Fingleton). The players were accused of drinking too much alcohol, keeping irregular hours, having poor fitness and not supporting the captain. Chairman Dr Allen Robertson advised the group that the allegations were not formal charges and as the meeting dispersed it was not lost on the group that what they shared in common was their background of Roman Catholicism – some suspected Bradman, a Protestant and Freemason to be behind it all.

Jack Fingleton and Bill O'Reilly had a well-documented dislike of Bradman, however Chuck Fleetwood-Smith and Stan

McCabe considered themselves close personal friends. In 2020, a Christmas 1935 greeting card from Don and Jessie Bradman to Stan and Edna McCabe was put up for auction. Accompanied with a studio portrait of the senders, the text was as follows:

> 'Thanks ever so much for your Xmas gift. So very kind and quite unnecessary. Our heartfelt greetings & wishes for a Merry Xmas and most prosperous 1936.
>
> Do you like us in the enclosed? We are not here but will serve to remind you of a couple of scallywags.
>
> Love to you all from us both.
>
> Truly yours,
>
> Don'

The Bradmans and McCabes often socialised together, Jessie and Edna becoming very close friends over games of bridge at the McCabe's Beauty Point home when the Bradmans visited Sydney. McCabe reportedly approached Bradman to ask whether he initiated the complaint against the five. Bradman emphatically denied it and was later informed by the Board that they had decided to take action without consulting with him.

As the sectarian divide now widened in the Australian Cricket Team, Oldfield began to get dragged into the 'Bradman camp' on account of his membership of the Freemasons and the Church of England – despite his own cool relations with Bradman. Jack Fingleton, in particular, habitually seemed to declare a conspiracy when anything in cricket did not go his way. In Greg Growden's 2008 biography of Fingleton were presented claims that Fingleton believed Oldfield, Bradman and Woodfull (a Methodist), formed a cabal to undermine his selection for the Australian team. He principally blamed them for him missing out on the 1934 tour of England despite being dropped from the Australian side for the final two Tests of the 1932-33 series after his 'pair' in Adelaide.

Fingleton took direct aim at Oldfield, quoted by Growden: "[t]hough he could be most charming and generally liked, most of us regarded him [Oldfield] with suspicion. He had a habit of asking mighty personal questions and we considered him a leaker of dressing-room gossip". Fingleton did not provide any evidence in support of the claim.

In his 1990 biography of Bill O'Reilly, author Jack McHarg was taken aback with his subject's opinion of Oldfield in which his own, "personal knowledge of Oldfield did not reveal any such character defects" and saying his personal dislike of him was "surprising". Believing that Oldfield's keeping had been in decline since 1935, particularly to Fleetwood-Smith, O'Reilly said the gloveman was good at covering-up his errors. Despite respecting his skill and career length, O'Reilly personally regarded Oldfield as an "insignificant man" and claimed that his opinion was formed as a result of his season in the New South Wales captaincy in which, according to him, newcomers were put through a "schoolboyish" initiation.

For someone like Oldfield, who was almost universally admired, Fingleton and O'Reilly's attitude towards him reinforces the adage that 'you can't please everyone'.

THE FINAL SESSION?

BACK IN KILLARA TO Ruth Mary's annoyance, the third Test of the 1936-37 season went into its sixth day on her seventh birthday. Waiting for her father when he arrived back from Melbourne was a wooden crate with a bicycle shipped from England for the birthday girl. Once home, Oldfield took the crate into the backyard to the excitement of the girls, but upon opening it, he found the item required almost complete assembly. Fortunately, a mechanically-minded friend passed by 'Poitiers' to assist with the detailed construction.

Oldfield would not be home for long following his unusual appointment as captain of a Combined Tasmania team which was scheduled to play the touring Englishmen in Hobart. Upon his return to Sydney, a Shield match awaited his services before the fourth Test in Adelaide at the end of January. Johnnie Moyes in the Sydney *Sun* of 13 January 1937, recognised the strain Oldfield was under due to the scheduling: "[a] wicket keeper is unlike any other player, for while on the field he cannot relax for a moment. His eyes must always be on the ball, and the nervous strain is therefore terrific". Moyes said Oldfield was "wise" in suggesting he may withdraw from the Shield match if selected for the Test team.

The problems arising from scheduling cricket matches have plagued administrators and players irrespective of the era. Excluding Don Bradman, the rest of the Australian Test players were due to play in the New South Wales versus Victoria match at the Sydney Cricket Ground, starting on 22 January and finishing on Anniversary Day (now Australia Day) – 3 days before the Adelaide Test. In the days of rail travel, the predicament was exacerbated. Victoria decided to field a full-strength side with all Test players while New South Wales excused their internationals, leaving Frank Easton to replace Oldfield. In the end, Victoria took first-innings points in the drawn match and won the Sheffield Shield that season.

After the mad dash to Adelaide, the Australian players quickly prepared themselves for the vital fourth Ashes Test. Len Darling and Frank Ward were dropped, and an unlucky Morris Sievers was replaced by state teammate Ernie McCormick who had recovered from injury. Oldfield may have been feeling his years after the selection of baby-faced Victorian youngster Ross Gregory, 20, who was born the year he was injured at Polygon Wood. Arthur Chipperfield returned to the side to bolster the batting.

Captain Bradman sent his team into bat after winning another toss. While most batsmen got starts, apart from McCabe (88) and Chipperfield (57 not out), none went on to capitalise and England's seamers dismissed the team for 288. O'Reilly (4 for 51) and Fleetwood-Smith (4 for 129) were again the main wicket-takers for Australia but England pushed ahead with a first innings total of 330 after a century from opener Charlie Barnett (129). Like the previous Melbourne Test, Australia reserved their best batting for the second innings after a successive Bradman double-century (212). In a heart-warming sight, promising debutant Ross Gregory walked arm-in-arm off the Adelaide Oval with his embattled captain at the end of the fourth day's play. Their crucial 135-run partnership was the highest in the Australian innings of 433, Gregory finished undefeated on 50. England again struggled with the peculiar variation of Fleetwood-Smith (6 for 110) on a worn wicket and fell on 243 runs – 148 short of victory. In spite of disastrous playing conditions and off-field controversy, Australia had clawed its way back from a near-fatal deficit to draw level in the series – 2-2.

Oldfield looks on as slip Arthur Chipperfield catches an edge from England batsman Maurice Leyland off Leslie Fleetwood-Smith in the fourth Test of the 1936-37 Ashes series.

Oldfield's experience of this Adelaide Test was in stark contrast to his ordeal four years before which resulted in him writhing on the floor of the dressing-room with a fractured skull, but concerns began to surface about his performance after a series of missed-stumpings, 18 byes leaked and two batting failures (5 and 1). Oldfield's much-admired former captain Bill Woodfull, now covering the Tests as a writer, addressed speculation that Oldfield should be replaced, declaring, "I do not consider that the time has come for Oldfield to step down...Oldfield is still our best keeper". In the event selectors did indeed decide to drop Oldfield, Woodfull nominated Ben Barnett over Don Tallon.

Back in Sydney, Oldfield's performances in the M.C.C. and South Australia matches helped his case for selection in the final Test with a catch, two stumpings and 30 not out in the New South Wales victory against the tourists and 2 catches a stumping and scores of 63 and 18 against the Croweaters. On 22 February 1937, it was confirmed that Oldfield had made the cut for the decider in Melbourne. In what may have been considered a bad omen, a motor vehicle's brakes failed on hilly Hunter Street and ploughed through the front window of his sports store while he was *en route* to the Test.

Gubby Allen walked gingerly off the Melbourne Cricket Ground having lost the toss for the third successive time to Don Bradman who was grinning ear-to-ear after electing to bat first. Dismissing openers Jack Fingleton and Keith Rigg, the Englishmen probably felt the Ashes slipping out of their reach as Bradman (169) and McCabe (112) took the score from 2 for 54 to 3 for 303 with surgical strokeplay. Jack Badcock was dropped by Gubby Allen off his own bowling to score a century (118) on his Test return.

After the fall of Badcock, Oldfield made his way to the crease to join a young man exactly half his age, Ross Gregory, who was celebrating his 21st birthday. The pair put on 19 runs before Gregory fended a Ken Farnes bouncer to veteran spinner Hedley Verity. Little did the old soldier at the non-striker's end know that all three of the men involved in the dismissal would die in a conflict set to engulf the world in a few short years.

All Australians, with the exception of O'Reilly, made double-figure contributions to the sizable total of 604. The demoralised Englishmen set about mounting a counter-offensive but were thwarted by recalled quick Laurie Nash (4 for 70) and Bill O'Reilly (5 for 51) to be dismissed for 239. Forced to follow-on, England collapsed to 165, handing Australia a victory by an innings and 200 runs – the Ashes were retained. Many in the press remarked that Oldfield's wicket-keeping in the Test was close to flawless, with two caught-behinds off Nash, a stumping off O'Reilly and no byes let through, on top of his 21 with the bat. If people were expecting a fairytale retirement announcement from Oldfield in the wake of an Ashes victory, they would be left disappointed. The little old keeper would keep-on keeping on.

Shortly after his return home, the Oldfields were dealt a blow with the death of the family's matriarch Mary following her passing at home in Lindfield on 17 March 1937, at the age of 85. A service was held in her honour at St Alban's Church, Lindfield before the funeral was conducted at Northern Suburbs Cemetery – many of Oldfield's teammates were in attendance.

As the winter of 1937 approached Oldfield's schedule was as hectic as ever. Causes assisting returned servicemen were particularly important to him and he devoted much time and resources in supporting them. A New South Wales Returned Services League sub-committee liaised with him on the structure of cricket competitions for war veterans. Oldfield held a fund-raiser for a New South Wales team of returned servicemen to tour Queensland, showing his films of the South Africa series for a shilling's admittance. In a prime position to souvenir stumps at the end of Test matches, he would often donate the memorabilia items to be used for fund-raising purposes. Oldfield gave a stump, signed by both teams from the fifth Test in Melbourne, to the

Bacchus Marsh R.S.L sub-branch which was auctioned for £52 ($4881) – the proceeds going towards aiding distressed veterans.

Apart from his women's teams, for a couple of years Oldfield had been sponsoring a men's side that would travel to play teams outside Sydney, including Moss Vale and Wollongong. In April, he joined his eponymous side for the first time in a match against Wisemans Ferry – playing as a bowler! The Oldfield's XI, which boasted future star Sid Barnes wearing the keeping gloves, defeated the local side with no wickets taken from the patron's right-arm slow offerings. George Borwick, the umpire at square-leg when he was struck in the head by Larwood at Adelaide, officiated in the match.

In its 1937 annual report, the Gordon District Cricket Club paid glowing tribute to the star they gladly accepted upon his move across the harbour 13 years before:-

> "Lucky, indeed, the team which boasts of Bertie Oldfield as one of its members. Not only because W.A.O. is 'Prince of Keepers', but because his ever gentlemanly demeanor [sic] makes him an ornament to the game and embellished the highest traditions of the sport. Probably the greatest complement ever paid to any wicket-keeper was that published by Umpire French of Sydney, who wrote: 'When Bertie appeals, an umpire could immediately declare the batsman out and inquire afterwards what had happened. To play more fairly than Bert would be impossible. He loves the game and his conscientious attitude at all times makes him an ideal model for all to copy".

Gordon would miss the early-season services of its famous keeper, with Oldfield's campaign to be selected for his fifth tour of England in 1938 commencing with his inclusion in a New South Wales regional touring team to the state's north. He celebrated his

43rd birthday in Grafton on the excursion which included matches against Maitland, Taree, Kempsey, Lismore and Casino across the month of September. Returning to grade cricket in the third round, he promoted himself to opener on a wet wicket at Trumper Park against Paddington to score 72 out of a 116 run partnership for the first wicket with Bob Hynes.

The 1937-38 Australian First-Class season started in November with the Sheffield Shield and a tour by the non-Test status New Zealanders. Without Test matches during the summer, Oldfield had a competitive field of state wicket-keepers to contend with for the Ashes tour. Having briefly flirted with retirement some years prior, the seasoned Charlie Walker was back for South Australia and Ben Barnett was building on years of experience with Victoria. Twenty-one-year-old Don Tallon had served his apprenticeship as Queensland gloveman and was being widely touted as an eventual Australian wicket-keeper.

Oldfield and Walker faced-off in the late-November Grimmett-Richardson testimonial match in Adelaide which exhibited the best 22 cricketers in the country and was viewed as an unofficial Ashes selection trial. Before announcing his retirement from all cricket, Richardson enjoyed one last victory over Bradman with his team eclipsing the Bradman XI's total in the drawn match. Oldfield scored 20 runs and took three caught-behinds in the match – two off his old collaborator Clarrie Grimmett.

After leading the dismissals table for the 1936-37 Sheffield Shield season with 14 catches and 4 stumpings, Oldfield's fate was sealed off the playing field. In Jack McHarg's biography of Bill O'Reilly, he records an encounter during the course of the mid-January match between New South Wales and South Australia in Sydney. With the 1938 Ashes touring team set to be named the following week, Australian captain and selector Don Bradman approached O'Reilly and asked him if he could pick him up from his lodgings on the way to the ground the next day – O'Reilly agreed. The following morning, in spite of the animosity that existed between the pair, Bradman sought O'Reilly's opinion on cricket matters, namely his thoughts on Oldfield. The feisty leg-spinner replied that in his opinion the keeper was "past it" – the veteran's fate was sealed.

On 27 January 1938, the Ashes team to England was announced and included the following players:-

Bradman (captain)
McCabe (vice-captain)
Badcock
Barnes
Brown
Chipperfield
Fingleton
Fleetwood-Smith
Hassett
McCormick
O'Reilly
Waite
Ward
White
Barnett (wicket-keeper)
Walker (back-up keeper)

For some, the omission of veteran players Oldfield and Grimmett was a shock – it was definitely the end of an era. As the news travelled around the cricketing world, eminent English cricket writer Neville Cardus, paid glowing tribute:

"[A]s to Oldfield, he has many friends in England who will be deploring that never again will they see Bertie walking down the pitch between overs flapping his gloves – that straight, neat walk – never again see him stump a man with the courtesy of a beau – Oldfield never bawled at the umpire, never gloated at the batsman's downfall. He did his destruction without rhetoric. Like the pirate in Byros he was always the gentleman – a sudden swoop, a flash of bail in the sunshine, and then we see Oldfield turning to the umpire. He left the roaring "H-zat" to his colleagues. I always imagined that Bertie himself was saying to the batsman: 'So sorry, but I had no choice. Law 23, you know. It should really be cancelled; not fair to take advantage behind a man's back. Still there it is; so sorry, see you again'. It must have been a pleasure to be stumped even in a Test match by Oldfield. We shall not look on his like again for many, many years. Frankly, I am sad about the passing over of Oldfield. Good judges of the game in Australia assure me that he is keeping as well as ever this season. That means he is the best keeper in the world".

Approached by the Sydney *Sun*, Oldfield admitted, "[i]t's no good saying I'm not disappointed…I never felt fitter for the job. I shall still be playing with my club and in other First-Class fixtures if selected this season". When asked about retirement he replied, "I'm still considering. I have not made up my mind". He confessed that it was, "hard to be cheerful at a moment like this but perhaps two who will be pleased that I am not going are my little daughters. I have had only two Christmases at home in 17 years and they'll see more of me now".

Wishing his old team the best, Oldfield said it appeared to have been selected with a view to blooding younger players, but expressed disappointment that youngster Ross Gregory had missed-out, as he had "proved that he has the temperament for Test cricket". The same newspaper launched the 'Bob-in For Bertie Fund' for cricket fans to express their gratitude to the long-serving player. Notable donors to the fund included New South Wales Premier Bertram Stevens, former Australian cricket captain Monty Noble and the Glebe District Cricket Club.

Oldfield's final First-Class appearance was for the match celebrating Australia's sesquicentenary held on the Sydney Cricket Ground between teams headed by Stan McCabe and Keith Rigg on 18-19 February 1938. Fittingly his final wicket was the McCabe XI's Sid Barnes, caught-behind off the bowling of his long-time teammate and fellow Test discard Clarrie Grimmett.

While he would eventually get more time to tend his dahlias at 'Poitiers' with the girls playing around him, Oldfield got to tour England in 1938, not as a player but as a journalist. He accepted offers from English newspaper the *Sunday Dispatch* and radio broadcasters to cover the Tests. He got to sit alongside his former captain Bill Woodfull in the press box and did not hold back on his opinions. Oldfield criticised Bradman's field placings during England's mammoth first Test innings of 8 declared for 658 which included centuries from Barnett (126), Hutton (100) and Compton (102) and a double-century from Eddie Paynter (216). Describing the fielding effort in general as "ragged", the erstwhile keeper said he had never seen an Australian team using their boots as much in an attempt to stop balls.

While in England as a correspondent Oldfield released his first book, *Behind the Wicket* in June 1938. Dedicated to his wife Ruth, he lists his career highlights and the best cricketers he played with and against, including chapters on the A.I.F. team and the major series he participated in, including Bodyline. Once again plagued by 4-day time-limited Test matches in England resulting in successive draws in the initial Tests, Oldfield was present to watch his old team retain the Ashes once again as they were victorious in the last three Tests.

After returning to Sydney following a short detour, Oldfield broadcast highlights of his observations during the 1938 Ashes on the city's Australian Broadcasting Commission station, 2BL. While crediting Bradman and O'Reilly with Australia's success, he warned that new players in key roles would be needed to defend the Ashes in the next home series. "We must face the facts, and realise that at least four or five new men are required in the next series", said Oldfield who singled-out McCormick as lacking stamina and Fleetwood-Smith and Ward for not consistently supporting O'Reilly in bowling partnerships. He warned that an England team with Len Hutton would bat very well on Australian soil and suggested that younger players like Don Tallon and Ross Gregory should be considered for future appointment to the Test arena.

While not making initial public comment on the performance of his replacement Ben Barnett, it was rumoured that he was not impressed with what he saw. Oldfield admitted that as a spectator to the Test matches, "[t]here were moments when I felt I must dash out on to the field and take my place behind the wickets. That feeling, I might say, still remains". During his 'Sidelights of the Australian Test matches' talks on 2BL, Oldfield was openly critical of Barnett. He claimed that while the Victorian's general work was acceptable, he failed to cooperate with the bowlers leading to poor results for the team. Following a backlash over his analysis, a surprised Oldfield defended himself saying his appraisal was, "based on actual facts".

At a homecoming reception in Adelaide, Bradman backed his new keeper against the criticisms: "Ben Barnett doesn't profess to be either a Hitler or an Oldfield. He is just an ordinary human being, like the rest of us". President of the Victorian Cricket

Association, the Reverend Canon Hughes, stated that Oldfield's criticisms of his state's wicket-keeper were unjustified and suggested that "silence was golden in such cases".

In amongst the news headlines of escalating global political tensions was Oldfield's formal announcement of his retirement from First-Class cricket on 2 November 1938. In a First-Class career spanning almost 19-years, he played in 245 matches taking 398 catches and 264 stumpings. He scored 6135 runs at an average of 23.70 an innings with 6 centuries and 21 half-centuries with a high score of 137.

Oldfield played in 54 of Australia's 68 Tests (79%) between the First and Second World Wars and was involved in every Test series played by Australia in the inter-war period apart from the 1938 Ashes series in England. Between the first Test of the 1924-25 Ashes series and the fifth test of the 1936-37 series, Oldfield only missed one match – the Brisbane Test of the 1932-33 Bodyline series – due to injury.

In his 17-year Test career, he played 54 matches, taking 78 catches and 52 stumpings and scored 1427 runs at an average of 22.60 with a high score of 65 not out. His career stumping tally remains a Test record after more than 80 years and is unlikely to be broken.

HOLIDAY IN NAZI GERMANY

On the way back home from reporting on the 1938 Ashes series in England, Oldfield took a detour to the capital city of his former foe, Berlin which was now emblazoned with Swastikas. Addresses on A.B.C. Radio and subsequent public lectures allowed him to convey his observations of the troubled European continent. Oldfield described his feeling of seeing the Reichstag building, which had been left dormant since a fire engulfed it in February 1933. He confessed to being, "deeply touched" by the once-grand building as "it stood in its homely magnificence unoccupied and unopened to the public, no longer a Parliament House, and to all intents and purposes completely useless".

Oldfield noticed the peculiar phenomenon: that physical education of youth had, "become a fetish or a religion in modern Germany", while in contrast he expressed compassion for his former enemy combatant as he observed the, "pitiful sight of old maimed soldiers charging people admission to buildings to see relics of the last war, and they see those relics with fear and trembling".

The now-retired Australian wicket-keeper was travelling through Nazi Germany during the Munich negotiations which were addressing German Chancellor Adolf Hitler's aggressive claims to the Sudetenland region of Czechoslovakia in September 1938. On the streets of Germany, he noticed an "absence of festivity and gaiety and a definite lack of humour". While there was a distinct "atmosphere of suspicion [reflected on] gloomy faces", the optimistic feedback he received from the average citizen was that there would be no war forthcoming from the crisis. Travelling through Austria, Hungary and Mussolini's Fascist Italy, people he spoke to felt the same, but as he travelled further east, those sentiments changed. "Czechoslovakia was the only exception" said Oldfield, "[t]he inhabitants lived from day to day in a fearful state of mind and expecting, hoping and praying for a peaceful settlement of the national problem". Oldfield confessed that irrespective of the feelings of the German people, "the decision whether there is war or not apparently does not rest with the German public, but with the Chancellor himself". So great was the overwhelming unease experienced during his European sojourn, Oldfield admitted to feeling great relief upon departure from Naples.

According to Hitler, the Sudetenland was the "last territorial demand" he sought to make in Europe and under the Munich Agreement, signed by leaders including British Prime Minister Neville Chamberlain and French Prime Minister Édouard Daladier in an attempt to appease the demands, the territory was assigned to Nazi Germany in early-October 1938. War had been averted...for now at least.

Retirement from First-Class cricket allowed the energetic Oldfield even more time to devote to assisting fellow ex-servicemen who were still not coping with life decades after the war had ended. As the honorary organiser of the War Veterans Home Art Union he launched an appeal to help fund the proposed War Veterans Home at Lake Narrabeen. He said there was still a proportion of "men of the A.I.F., dejected, despondent and very much in need of encouragement and comfort". The proposed facility aimed to provide, "free medical, dental and nursing attention to these worthy citizens, who valiantly fought for the Empire and who are now suffering as a result of service abroad".

In a cruel blow for the old keeper, he was unable to reprise his role in an A.I.F. Cricket Team reunion match in Melbourne in April 1939, owing to a broken finger. Hammy Love was his understudy once again as the Herbie Collins-led team went down by 4 wickets to the younger 'Old Internationals' team which included Arthur Mailey, Charlie Macartney, Alan Kippax, Bill Ponsford and Clarrie Grimmett. Proceeds of the match, attended by 9000 spectators, went to the War Veterans' Fund.

BACK IN THE SLOUCH HAT

Explaining to others that retirement from cricket had left a "big gap" in his life, Oldfield enlisted as a private in the 17th Infantry Battalion of the Australian Military Forces, the 80,000-strong citizen militia, on 3 May 1939. Awaiting his medical examination a week later, the 44-year-old told the Sydney *Sun* that he had, "no fear of being turned down as I have never felt fitter in my life". After gaining an appendectomy scar and putting on less than a kilogram since 1915 – he was back in military service. By August, he was promoted to his former rank of corporal and a month later, elevated to sergeant. Oldfield's new duties still allowed him to swap the slouch hat for the baggy maroon of the Gordon club at the weekend.

Since he had returned from Europe, the Nazi leadership in Germany had not been satisfied with gaining the Sudetenland and proceeded to annex the Czech region of Czechoslovakia in March 1939. The German invasion of Poland on 1 September was the last straw for the United Kingdom and France with both powers declaring war on 3 September and Prime Minister Robert Menzies announcing Australia's participation the following day. The ensuing week included the federal government's implementation

Oldfield wearing the uniform of the Australian Military Forces in 1939.

of new national security measures and imposition of press censorship for the duration of the war. In a nation which had barely recovered from the First World War and had been ravaged by the Depression for a decade, it was once again mobilising scarce resources for the new global conflict. In consultation with the British government, Prime Minister Menzies pledged a military contribution of 100,000 men to the Allied war effort. The Australian 6th Division had been formed in late-1939 and embarked for Egypt to undergo further training with a view to deployment in Europe, but France was to fall to Nazi Germany following the British evacuation of Dunkirk the next year.

As a result of the growing turmoil the benefit match for Bert Oldfield and Alan Kippax, slated for 2 – 5 December 1939 at the Sydney Cricket Ground was postponed indefinitely. As a consolation the long-time wicket-keeper and former captain was elected a life member of the New South Wales Cricket Association.

On 23 November 1939, Oldfield was commissioned as a lieutenant attached to the Eastern Command Headquarters where he would be utilised in administration and training of troops. The newly-minted commissioned officer used his influence and contacts to organise a match between the old A.I.F. and the new 2nd A.I.F. at Trumper Park, Paddington on 4 January 1940 to aid the Comfort's Fund. Ruth Oldfield was in prestigious company, flanked by Lieutenant-General Sir Thomas Blamey and Governor General Lord Gowrie as they watched the original A.I.F. team win by 3 wickets. Fifty-year-old Herbie Collins returned as captain along with Hammy Love, Charlie Macartney, Johnny Taylor and Charlie Kelleway. The highlight of the match was Macartney's innings of 81 runs and 3 wickets for 38 at the age of 53. Oldfield performed well with two stumpings, a catch and 16 not out. The match, which raised total funds of £77 ($6600), ended on a poignant note with the players gathering together on the ground to sing *'Auld Lang Syne'*.

In honour of his military and cricket service, the Blacktown

Council in western Sydney announced in March 1940 that they would be naming a new road after the former Australian keeper. Oldfield Road would link Seven Hills Road and Wall Park Avenue in the burgeoning residential suburb of Seven Hills. Enjoying a city luncheon with Ruth before going into camp, Oldfield was chosen to be an instructor for the refresher course for re-enlisting Great War veterans like himself at the training camp set-up at Randwick Racecourse between 8 July 1940 and 17 August 1940.

Australian troops were pivotal in the capture of the Libyan towns of Bardia and Tobruk from Italian forces to establish an Allied garrison in North Africa in January 1941. Increasingly, it seemed that tanks would be critical for the Allied war effort and the 1st Armoured Division was formed. Lieutenant Oldfield enlisted with the permanent forces joining the 2nd A.I.F., assigned to the fledgling tank corps on 16 April 1941 under the serial number NX429 with a potential for overseas deployment. From September 1941, he briefly relocated to Victoria to serve on the staff of the Armoured Division's commander General John Northcott and played as wicket-keeper for the Hawthorn-East Subdistrict XI on his days off. After performing staff duties for most of 1941, including as acting-Captain, Oldfield resumed his training role following the announcement of a reconstructed Volunteer Defence Corp which would perform the role of a Home Guard. For almost 12-months, Oldfield was on the staff of the training camp based at the Kembla Grange racecourse in the Illawarra region south of Sydney – achieving the full rank of Captain during that time.

While the initial focus of the Australian response to the unfolding global conflict was confrontation with Nazi Germany and its allies, Japan increasingly came into play as a growing threat in the Pacific region. In late 1941, new Labor Prime Minister John Curtin ordered the 9th Division, which had courageously weathered the siege on Tobruk by Axis forces, to return to Australia. On 7 December 1941, Japanese air forces attacked the United States naval base at Pearl Harbour, plunging the region into a state of war. With an Australian militia battalion already based in Port Moresby, units of the 8th Division were deployed to Ambon and Timor anticipating Japan's drive into South-East Asia. That incursion came in early 1942 upon the Japanese capturing the port of Rabaul in New Britain in January and the catastrophic fall of the strategic British outpost of Singapore to Japanese forces in February. Utilising their aircraft carriers and an advanced foothold in the Dutch East-Indies, the Japanese launched an aerial attack on Darwin on 19 February 1942 causing severe casualties and destruction. By March, the Japanese had established bases in New Guinea, including Lae, and had reached the Solomon Islands, while in May midget submarines attacked naval shipping in Sydney Harbour – war was on Australia's doorstep.

By July 1942, the Imperial Japanese Army increased their foothold in the north of New Guinea and pushed inland where they ran into Australian troops near the village of Kokoda. A ferocious tug-of-war in the jungle-covered Owen Stanley mountain range continued over the ensuing months until the Japanese withdrew to pockets on the northern coastline.

The threat of an invasion of the Australian mainland having abated, the 1st Armoured Division was disbanded opening a new role for Oldfield. On 27 September 1942, Army Minister Frank Forde announced his appointment to the position of sport staff-officer in the Australian Army Amenities Service. The amenities section, which in addition to sport, involved radio services and entertainment for deployed troops. Having been the beneficiary of similar efforts in the First World War which launched his cricket career, the role was a good fit for Oldfield who was promoted to

Major on 9 July 1943. He became the central figure in the creation of the Services Cricket Team which involved organising matches between the Services and state teams for the cricket-starved public, benefitting the Comfort's Fund.

After defeats at Gona and Buna over New Year 1943, the defiant Japanese continued to be rooted-out of north-eastern New Guinea by Australian and United States forces. Later in the year, Allied troops had landed in Bougainville and New Britain and continued to make further gains in New Guinea well into 1944. The Royal Australian Air Force and Oldfield's Australian Army Amenities Service launched radio services to inform and entertain battle-weary and homesick troops. Catering for both American and Australian troops, 9PA Port Moresby (later 9AA) was opened by U.S. General Douglas McArthur and Australian Broadcasting Commission director-general Sir Charles Moses on 26 February 1944. Broadcasting in morning, lunchtime and evening blocks, the programming on 9AA included local content and relayed news from the A.B.C. and American Armed Forces Radio services.

Despite the tide turning against them in the South Pacific, the Japanese held onto their gains fiercely and would need to be chiselled out of every corner they occupied. The final phase of dislodging Japanese forces involved taking Wewak on the New Guinea mainland and the island of Bougainville to the east, in early 1945. While Allied troops were still fighting the island's garrison of 2500 Japanese, the Amenities Service set-up a radio station at the military base at Torokina.

As news spread across the world of the death of Adolf Hitler and the imminent end of the conflict in Europe, Major Oldfield's war was not over as he embarked from Sydney on the *Montoro* to Bougainville on 4 May 1945. After stopping-off in the newly-secured New Guinea coastal village of Aitepe, he arrived in

Major Bert Oldfield (right) shakes the hand of Lieutenant Miller of the U.S. Marine Aircraft Wing at Torokina, Bougainville, 1945.

Bougainville on 6 July. As the Amenities chief, Oldfield put together a program of competitive sports from badminton to rugby league to keep the troops occupied and coached a little bit of cricket when time permitted. A coup for the service was securing world famous British entertainer Gracie Fields to perform a concert for the troops on Bougainville. Recovering from cancer surgery and a marriage breakdown, Fields was displaced from her home on the Isle of Capri due to the war and signed-on with the Entertainments National Service Association. She sang her wartime anthem *'Wish Me Luck as You Wave Me Goodbye'* to troops across Britain and France, mixing comedy and music hall, delivered with her signature Lancastrian charm. Major Oldfield cheekily grabbed an autograph from Fields in the backstage tent before the Torokina concert on 8 August 1945 where she was supported by Australian vocalist Peggy Shea.

During Fields's visit to Bougainville, reports arrived on the island of a terrifying new weapon – the atomic bomb. Capable of destroying an entire city, it had been unleashed on the Japanese port of Hiroshima by American bombers. Armed with the intelligence that the enemy hidden away on the volcanic island were listening, the 9AC Torokina radio service broadcast news of Hiroshima and the following atomic bombing of Nagasaki in the Japanese language.

After significant combat casualties and the impact of tropical disease, the Japanese resistance on Bougainville broke in late-August with pockets of depleted units surrendering across the island. The formal surrender of Bougainville came on 8 September 1945 – six days after the Japanese unconditional capitulation to the Allied forces. Oldfield's most vivid memory of Gracie Fields's time on the island was not the concert, but a thanksgiving service where she sang *'The Lord's Prayer'* to 15,000 troops. "It was the most solemn scene I have ever witnessed" he recalled, "[a]ll around me were battle-stained troops, many with tears in their eyes".

Leaving Torokina in early October, Oldfield travelled on the *Taroona*, disembarking in Brisbane a fortnight later. After arriving back in Sydney, he immediately took the family for holiday in the N.S.W. Southern Highlands and performed assistant church warden duties at St Jude's Church, Bowral – the Bradman family's church where a young Don had sung in the choir.

Apart from the global impact, the Second World War had a devastating bearing on the cricket world and the Australian wicket-keeping fraternity was not spared. Oldfield's 1930 Ashes understudy Charlie Walker was killed when his Avro Lancaster was shot down over Soltau, Germany on 17 December 1942 at the age of 33. Oldfield's Test replacement Ben Barnett, was serving as a signaller during the Fall of Singapore and was a prisoner-of-war for 3-and-a-half years. Fed only rice gruel by his captors for those years and having suffered from malaria and beri-beri, Barnett

Major Bert Oldfield requests the autograph of entertainer Gracie Fields who performed for the troops with opera singer Peggy Shea (left), Torokina, Bouainville, 1945.

survived the deprivations of Changi prison and forced labour on the Thai-Burma Railway.

The participants in the dismissal 'Gregory c. Verity b. Farnes 80' in the fifth Ashes Test in 1937, which Oldfield witnessed from the non-striker's end, were killed within 2 years of each other. Ken Farnes, a pilot officer, died shortly after take-off from an air-strip in Oxfordshire on 20 October 1941, age 30. Ross Gregory, also a pilot officer, died on 10 June 1942 when his bomber crashed in East Bengal – he was aged 26. Captain Hedley Verity was mortally wounded by shrapnel while leading troops in Caserta, Italy on 31 July 1943, at the age of 38.

Oldfield was discharged from the 2nd A.I.F. on the rank of Major on 12 March 1946 and was awarded the Pacific Star, British War Medal and the Australian Service Medal.

TO THE CLOSE OF PLAY

THE UNCERTAINTY AND SEPARATION of the war years were compounded for the Oldfield family with personal tragedies. In 1942, Oldfield's elder sister Lyle Sattler died, survived by husband Tony and daughters Merle and Enid. Tony Sattler, who managed Oldfield's city sports store, subsequently married one of Bert's other sisters, Linda. Ruth Oldfield's mother, Maud, died in 1943 at the age of 64 survived by her husband John.

Early in the war, daughter Ruth Mary aged 10 at the time, had been knocked-down and dragged by a car while the Oldfields had been holidaying in the Blue Mountains town of Medlow Bath and suffered a compound leg fracture, back abrasions and a head injury. Her daughter Karin Sussmann describes what she knows of the incident, "she nearly lost her leg. The doctor was brilliant and saved her leg, it was hanging on by a ligament and he stitched it all back together. She was concussed and dragged along by the car for some time. They used to go up to Medlow Bath for holidays and she was crossing the road there. She had a huge scar around her leg on the lower half".

Having made a full recovery apart from life-long scarring, Ruth Mary spent much of the war as a boarding student at the

Presbyterian Ladies College in rural Orange. Following in her father's footsteps, she was a very keen cricketer and played in the school XI. While only having a passing interest in cricket, Judith Ann's attentions were more artistic as she expressed hopes of becoming a pianist in the future.

Retirement from cricket and army service allowed Oldfield more time to devote to church duties. Since moving to the North Shore, he had attended St Martin's Anglican Church, Killara, and undertook the lay ministry role as a sidesman- an assistant church warden's position which included greeting parishioners at the door, overseeing seating arrangements and taking-up the collection. Oldfield consistently spoke against the playing of organised sport on the Sabbath but felt it was acceptable for informal games being played on Sunday afternoons.

In the years following the war, Oldfield continued to organise cricket matches to raise funds for Legacy to assist the families of fallen soldiers and was pivotal in the Australian fundraising efforts for veteran English cricketers Phil Mead and Len Braund who were both suffering from medical issues. Karin Sussmann recalls of her grandfather: "Bert was very involved in Legacy and he would have us sell the buttons door-to-door after school. He was very involved in the community and did a lot for others. He was very involved, he was involved in three Masonic Lodges: the Grand Lodge, Cricket Lodge and the local Roseville Lodge. He was very community-minded".

Having retired from grade cricket, he continued keeping wicket for the Gordon Veterans team and increasingly added coaching sessions to his regional lecture tours.

In 1946, Oldfield ended his association with the Australian Broadcasting Commission after signing a contract with Sydney radio station 2GB to commentate on the 1946-47 Ashes series in Australia, joining Jack Fingleton, Victor Richardson and Bill Woodfull who added their voices to cricket broadcasting.

Tragedy struck the Oldfields again with the death of Tony Sattler who died suddenly of a heart attack when about to play a round of snooker at home in Lindfield on 28 September 1948, aged 60. Having only been married to Linda for a couple of years the loss of his trusted management of the sports store would be a double blow for Oldfield.

During 1948, the New South Wales Cricket Association floated the possibility of an Oldfield – Kippax testimonial match, which had been originally scheduled for early-December 1939. Controversy arose when the South Australian Cricket Association proposed a benefit match for Don Bradman in Melbourne sometime during the 1948-49 season. The New South Wales Cricket Association objected to the Bradman match arguing that the Oldfield-Kippax match had been postponed for almost a decade and that two testimonial matches in the season would amount to saturation. In England during the 1948 'Invincibles' Ashes tour, Bradman was contacted by Arthur Mailey writing in the *Daily Telegraph*. When asked about the New South Wales Cricket Association's objections to his benefit match, Bradman said the matter was completely out of his hands and when Mailey enquired whether he would play in the Oldfield-Kippax match, he curtly replied, "[y]ou have already heard me say in public I have definitely retired from First-Class cricket". Despite the impasse, both matches went ahead with Bradman's match played at the Melbourne Cricket Ground in which he entertained the crowd with 123 and in-kind received a £10,000 ($570,000) benefit.

After all the toing-and-froing, a newly-knighted Sir Donald Bradman agreed to be the drawcard of the Oldfield – Kippax testimonial match at the Sydney Cricket Ground over February

A program from the Kippax-Oldfield Testimonial Concert which was held at the Sydney Town Hall in conjunction with the testimonial match.

and March 1949, in what would be his penultimate First-Class cricket appearance. In 2020, rare footage shot on colour film capturing part of Bradman's innings of 53 was unearthed and released by the Australian National Film and Sound Archive. Bert Oldfield and Alan Kippax went home with £3015 ($172,000) each from their match. The days of the traditional testimonial matches would eventually become numbered in favour of a player pension scheme as it was argued that wet weather could potentially ruin fund-raising efforts.

Oldfield's loyalty may have come into question in some quarters when agreeing to provide coaching for the touring England Women's Cricket Team prior to playing a Molly Dive-led New South Wales in 1948. English wicket-keeper Betty Snowball and her two back-ups soaked-up Oldfield's advice: "[w]e talked for a while and then I showed them a few points on keeping technique" he said. His right eye may have twitched slightly when hearing of fast bowler Mary Johnson's nickname – the 'Larwood of Women's Cricket'.

Surprising news broke in 1950 with Harold Larwood selling his Blackpool sweet shop to permanently relocate his family to Australia. In an announcement reported in the *Truth* of 12 February, Larwood informed his "old pals in Australia" that he intended to settle down in the country, "I have five daughters...so you see it will be a big thing for me to do, but I have a longing to return". Larwood moved into a house in the south-eastern Sydney suburb of Kingsford across the harbour from Oldfield. Reunited through a series of professional and social events – the former combatants became unlikely friends. Only weeks after arriving in Australia, Oldfield had arranged an office assistant's position for Larwood's eldest daughter, 20-year-old June with Olympic athletics official Hugh Weir.

As members of the travelling press corps covering the 1950-51 Ashes series; Larwood writing for an English newspaper and Oldfield commentating for radio – the pair formed a warm bond. Adelaide *Mail* journalist Lawrie Jervis Jr, during a break in the M.C.C. – South Australia tour match, caught the men in a quiet moment in stark contrast to the hostility of 18-years prior, reporting: "who should be chatting quietly, reminiscently, and smilingly in the Adelaide Oval members' stand before the...game resumed, but Larwood and Bertie Oldfield. You've never seen two people in such a jovial huddle". The old warriors were named in the same side for a charity match in Melbourne organised by Bill Ponsford on Christmas Eve 1950. The 'Empire Writers' team, which brought together former Ashes competitors including Bill O'Reilly, Bill Bowes and Victor Richardson, played a Ponsford team to aid the Premature Babies' Ward at the Queen Victoria Memorial Hospital. In the end, 46-year-old Larwood offered to umpire the match, presumably to avoid re-aggravating his front foot problems.

An extraordinary gathering occurred in the restaurant of Sydney's Pickwick Club on 14 January 1954, initiated by writer and cartoonist Arthur Mailey. The former Australian leg-spinner who worked for the *Daily Telegraph* newspaper organised a Bodyline reunion lunch which was attended by Douglas Jardine, Harold Larwood, Bert Oldfield and his close friends Charlie Macartney, Johnny Taylor and Warren Bardsley. To complete the high-level gathering, Australian Prime Minister Robert Menzies was in attendance at the lunch table. In the country on business, Jardine confessed that he did not expect anybody in Australia would be prepared to invite him for lunch. When asked how he would have confronted Bodyline bowling, Macartney declared that he would have, "[b]elted the cover off it". Prime Minister Menzies reportedly shamed the rest of those assembled at the table with his cricket knowledge.

As the group bade each other farewell, Jardine shook his former spearhead's hand saying, "goodbye Harold, it's been lovely to see you". Larwood warmly replied, "come back and see me again, skipper". It would be the last time they would meet -Jardine dying of cancer in 1958. Sadly, Warren Bardsley died a week later at his Collaroy home, aged 70. Paying tribute, Oldfield said he would never forget Bardsley's brilliant batting performances in England.

In the early 1950s the Oldfield girls, now young women, sought about making their own mark on the world. At the age of 21, Ruth completed her training as a Tresillian nurse, specialising in mother-crafting. Motivated by her artistic interests, Judith relocated to Italy to attend the Florence School of Fine Arts at the Villa Schipanola where she specialised in oil painting. Still passionate about music, Judith made the most of Europe, travelling to music festivals in Salzburg, Bayreuth and Edinburgh.

Ruth Oldfield accompanied both her daughters on journeys to Ceylon staying in Colombo with friends that Bert had made on previous stop-overs on Ashes tour voyages. It would be on one

Former combatants Bert Oldfield and Harold Larwood share a laugh at a lunch with former England captain Douglas Jardine and Prime Minister Robert Menzies at Sydney's Pickwick Club in 1954.

of the voyages to Ceylon that Ruth Mary would meet her future husband, Jacques Sussmann. Sussmann came from a family of Austro-Ukrainian jewellers, watch and spectacle makers which had settled in the Egyptian capital of Cairo some years prior. As a result of the 1952 revolution in Egypt which saw the toppling of the monarchy by nationalist military officers led by Gamal Abdel Nasser, it became increasingly uncomfortable for Westerners in the country and Sussman was tasked by his father to investigate Australia as a migration option.

Jacques Sussmann and Ruth Mary Oldfield were married in 1952, with their first child Karin born in 1953, four more children would follow: Karl, Gretchen, Konrad and Rebekah.

Now a grandfather, Oldfield often found the tranquillity of his home in Killara taken-up with babysitting duties. Karin recalls, "we had fun with him sometimes, but the circumstances with the family were that he sometimes was inundated with kids, he was a bit old and beyond having naughty, noisy kids around. We'd go there and we'd all pile into my grandmother's bed when we stayed there in the holidays and he'd come in with morning tea. He would always bring my grandmother a cup of tea at 7 o'clock in the morning and we'd have milky tea with fairy bread".

Of her grandfather, Karin believes his military service shaped him as a man, but he never discussed the war with his grandchildren: "we used to go to the shop with him in the school holidays and we would have to walk like we were in the army, chest out, back straight. Formality was important, cleaning your shoes was important, you used to have to see your face in the shine. He never mentioned the war to us, we were just the grandchildren and we wouldn't have known anything about the war. It was not of any interest to us as young kids. We didn't live it, we didn't know much about it. I know he was in both World Wars.

In the First World War, I knew he got into playing for [the A.I.F. team] because he was injured and in convalescence in England. He got an opportunity to play and they saw how good he was".

Of his cricketing career, Oldfield spoke very little to his grandchildren mostly Karin believes out of modesty: "we didn't know anything about his career while he was alive, that would have been a bragging thing. He didn't have conversations with us. He used to take us to games at the Sydney Cricket Ground. They were hoping that Karl would follow in his footsteps when he joined the Gordon club at Chatswood".

Oldfield released his second book in 1954, *The Rattle of the Stumps*. Foreworded by Sir Jack Hobbs, the work is less autobiographical than 1938's *Behind the Wicket*, with more of an instructional focus and commentary on cricket issues. Unlike many books at the time that were used for score-settling, Oldfield chose to be uncontroversial, preferring to praise the performances of modern players, particularly England's Len Hutton, and making suggestions on ways to brighten the game.

In 1958, Oldfield's friend of almost 40-years: business partner, fellow Freemason and teammate in all tiers of cricket – Charlie 'The Governor General' Macartney, passed away at the age of 72. Arthur Mailey, one of Australian cricket's brightest characters and Oldfield stumping collaborator died just short of his 82nd birthday on New Year's Eve, 1967. Johnny Taylor: Oldfield's best-man, teammate and travelling companion died in Turramurra at the age of 75 on 12 May 1971.

Into his 70s, Oldfield continued coaching schoolboys teams, and following a conversation with Ethiopian emperor Haile Selassie, undertook a groundbreaking coaching tour of the African nation in 1964. The series of overseas tours that were initiated by Oldfield formed the basis of the Australian Schoolboys Cricket

Council. The Council oversaw the introduction of interstate schoolboys Cricket Week carnivals in Australia.

Changing trends in the Sydney central business district led to the northern end of the city transforming into a financial district, resulting in Oldfield moving his Hunter Street store into a more retail-friendly location at 243 Pitt Street after 43 years at the previous site. The basement shop was opened in May 1965 by radio and television personality Eric Baume and reflected Oldfield's own tidy and ordered nature with neat displays of sporting items. In the new shop, Oldfield set-up a 'glory wall' of his cricketing achievements which included his famed Hobbs catch and stumping from 1924-25 and beautiful photographic study of him keeping up to the stumps as Walter Hammond strikes a perfectly balanced cover-drive. The following year he was interviewed in front of the wall for a documentary about Sir Donald Bradman and the seasoned raconteur delivered a seamless monologue of his recollections of the young Don's rise to prominence. After serving on coaching panels and continuing to attend matches through the 1960s, Oldfield was named an Honoured Member of the Order of the British Empire for services to cricket in the Queen's Birthday honours list of 8 June 1970.

THE FINAL ACCOUNT

Bert Oldfield and Harold Larwood were an unlikely pairing. Enemy combatants at the flashpoint of the acrimonious Bodyline series, in which one had fractured the skull of the other with a cricket ball over 40 years earlier, were now close friends. Approaching his 82nd birthday the following month, on Monday 9 August 1976, Oldfield had arranged to have lunch with his old mate Larwood in the city during the week, something that the pair had been doing regularly since the mid-1950s, commencing with the jovial Bodyline reunion with Douglas Jardine at the Pickwick Club in 1954.

Despite being in his 80s, Oldfield was still working every day in the sports store that he had established over half-a-century prior. For decades he walked from his home in Springdale Road, Killara to catch the North Shore railway line into the city to the Pitt Street store, but now on occasions his store manager Claude Earl would pick him up in his vehicle and drive him across the Sydney Harbour Bridge to work.

He had returned home to 'Poitiers' on the Monday night after a day's work in the shop but it would not be home for much longer. The Oldfields had decided to downsize, had purchased a unit in the nearby suburb of Roseville and were in the process of moving out having sold their home of 45 years. The spritely octogenarian would retire to his bed for the night in much the same way as every other night to build-up his energy reserves for the following day.

For some time, unbeknownst to the cricket world and the general public, Bert Oldfield had been suffering regular epileptic seizures which had developed later in his life. The seizures were so frequent that Ruth Oldfield would be on alert to respond when an episode of fitting occurred – making sure that he would not injure himself on objects during his convulsions and ensuring he was placed in the recovery position following the seizure. Karin Sussmann recalls: "my grandmother would get up after hearing him have a fit and make sure that he didn't swallow his tongue".

Oldfield had not been diagnosed with congenital epilepsy in his early life but appeared to have acquired the neurological disorder. He had sustained a number of serious traumatic brain injuries throughout his lifetime: on the battlefield and on the cricket field – most notably at the Battle of Polygon Wood in 1917 and at the Adelaide Oval during the Bodyline series in 1933. Post-traumatic seizures are known to occur soon after, but sometimes years following the initial injury.

It had become a joke in modern times that in the sport of cricket protection of the male genitalia had preceded protection of the brain as a matter of priority – by a whole century. Oldfield having played his entire cricketing career helmet-less, the sport only started to tentatively explore the idea of head protection in the 1970s – four decades after he had retired from the Test arena.

Typically moving at a snail's pace in relation to player welfare and safety, cricket has adopted a series of concussion protocols for participants who sustain knocks to the head. Sportsmen in football codes such as rugby league and American football have been diagnosed with Chronic Traumatic Encephalopathy (CTE), a neurodegenerative disease linked to repeated head-knocks with the onset of the disease developing in middle age – sometimes earlier.

Karin Sussmann says the Oldfield family believed that Bert's condition was acquired as a soldier, "it was possibly brought-on because of asphyxiation, the fact that he was buried during the war and possibly because of cricket as well". The family would approach the Department of Veterans Affairs at the time believing that his war injuries were partially responsible for his condition, however the authorities were initially dismissive.

On the morning of Tuesday 10 August 1976, Ruth Oldfield awoke in the Killara home she was soon to vacate to begin her daily routine. She noticed that Bert was not his busy self, getting ready for another day in the sports store. An unusual quiet had descended on 'Poitiers'. Upon investigation, she found her husband of 47 years lifeless in his room, having suffered a seizure overnight. Bert Oldfield had passed away at the age of 81.

Karin Sussmann recalls the day of her grandfather's passing: "I went overseas in '75, I do remember being given the information that he had died, I had been living overseas but I came back and I was living in a place that didn't have a phone. Family came and gave me a message that he had passed".

Upon hearing of Oldfield's death, a crestfallen Harold Larwood described him as, "a real gentleman on and off the field. We were to have lunch together tomorrow. I just can't say how shocked I am".

In the *Canberra Times* of the following day, former teammate Jack Fingleton who now worked as a federal political correspondent, had evidently softened his opinion of Oldfield over the years, describing him as "peerless". Fingleton said, "Bertie Oldfield was one of cricket's immortals...[a]t his top he was the greatest wicket-keeper in the world, neat, dapper, stylish and dependable".

Oldfield's funeral was held at St Martins Anglican Church, Killara where he served for many years as a sidesman, and was buried alongside his parents-in-law John and Maud Hunter in their family plot in the Church of England section at Rookwood Cemetery in Sydney.

Following his death, Ruth Oldfield moved into the Roseville unit which the couple had purchased and younger daughter Judith, who remained unmarried throughout her life, moved-in with her mother. Ruth lived a full and active life in the years following Bert's death and was visited frequently by her eldest daughter, Ruth. Karin Sussmann says, "she and her mother were very close, they had a very tight relationship – codependent. She used to come down and take her out a couple of times a week. Take her shopping and then they'd sit and have lunch together in a café where they were well-known".

After suffering from a number of falls, hospital admissions and stints in rehabilitation later in life, Ruth Oldfield passed away on 16 August 2009 at the remarkable age of 101. Her death had a profound effect on Ruth, Karin Sussmann recalls: "she went downhill rapidly once her mother, Ruth senior, died a month before her 102nd birthday. My mother was 79 at the time and even then she just went downhill. When she didn't have that relationship anymore she deteriorated quite a lot".

Judith Oldfield passed away peacefully at home in Sydney on 15 May 2019 at the age of 87. Her funeral was held at St Martins Anglican Church in Killara and she was buried in the same cemetery as her father at Rookwood.

Ruth Mary Sussman (nee Oldfield) moved into an aged care facility on the Queensland Sunshine Coast where she suffered from dementia in the last years of her life. She passed away on 19 May 2022, aged 92.

Interest in the 1932-33 Ashes series was reignited in 1984 with the airing of the television mini-series *Bodyline* on the Ten Network. Produced by Kennedy Miller, the production company of George Miller and Byron Kennedy of *Mad Max* fame – the seven episode series was made a year after the well-received *The Dismissal* which chronicled the demise of the Whitlam Government in 1975. The role of Bert Oldfield was played by actor Les Dayman who had previously appeared in the film *Gallipoli* and television police dramas *Division 4* and *Homicide*. In much the same way as the real events, Oldfield being struck in the head in the Adelaide Test was the tense, dramatic crescendo of the dramatisation. Despite Harold Larwood's objection to his portrayal and Sir Donald Bradman's dismissive critique, a significant viewership tuned into the series which provoked a nostalgia for 1930s cricket and a resurgence of interest in the Bodyline series, the Bradman era and the 1948 Invincibles tour for the next decade and beyond.

Around the 1990s, just a stone's throw from Oldfield's former property in Springdale Road, Killara, the picket-fenced oval on the picturesque Killara Park was renamed the W.A. Bert Oldfield Oval and is still used for third and fourth grade matches by his beloved Gordon District Cricket Club.

On Oldfield Road, Seven Hills a public school was built in 1959 and for decades was simply known as the Oldfield Road Public School. In 1988, the New South Wales government renamed the school in the cricketer's honour – the motto chosen for the Bert Oldfield Public School was 'Learn to Live'. For generations of students who have had the privilege of attending the school and having its motto emblazoned over their hearts, there could be no

The W.A. 'Bert' Oldfield Oval, Killara.

greater example than the man who lived every moment of his life to the absolute fullest.

THE END

W.A. OLDFIELD PLAYING RECORD

First-Class debut: 29 May 1919, Australian Imperial Force v Oxford University, Oxford

Test debut: 17 December 1920, 1st Test Australia v England, Sydney Cricket Ground

Final Test: 26 February 1937, 5th Test Australia v England, Melbourne Cricket Ground

Final First-Class match: 18 February 1938, KE Rigg's XI v SJ McCabe's XI, Sydney Cricket Ground

Test Statistics

Matches	Innings	Runs	High Score	50/100	Average	Strike Rate	Ct/St
54	80	1427	65*	4/-	22.60	37	78/51

First-Class Statistics

Matches	Innings	Runs	High Score	50/100	Average	Strike Rate	Ct/St
245	315	6135	137	21/6	23.70	-	398/264

BIBLIOGRAPHY

Books

Bean, Charles Edwin Woodrow, *Official History of Australia in the Great War, Vol.IV. The A.I.F in France 1917*, Angus and Robertson, Sydney 1943

Cardwell, Ronald, *The AIF Cricket Team*, R. Cardwell, Sydney 1980

Frith, David, *Archie Jackson: The Keats of Cricket*, Pavilion, London 1987

Geddes, Margaret, *Remembering Bradman*, Viking, Melbourne 2003

Growden, Greg, *Jack Fingleton: The Man Who Stood Up To Bradman*, Allen and Unwin, Sydney 2008

Jardine, Douglas, *In Quest of the Ashes*, Rigby, Adelaide 1984

Larwood, Harold, *Body-Line?*, Elkin Mathew & Marrot, London 1933

Larwood, Harold with Perkins, Kevin, *The Larwood Story*, Allen, London 1965

McGilvray, Alan, *The Game is Not the Same*, ABC, Sydney 1985

McHarg, Jack, *Bill O'Reilly: A Cricketing Life. The Authorised Biography*, Millenium, Sydney 1990

Oldfield, William Albert Stanley, *Behind the Wicket*, Hutchinson & Co, London 1938

Oldfield, William Albert Stanley, *The Rattle of the Stumps*, George Newnes Ltd, London 1954

Page, Michael, *Bradman – the Illustrated Biography*, Macmillian, Melbourne 1983

Piesse, Ken and Davis, Charles, *Encyclopedia of Australian Cricket Players*, New Holland, Sydney 2012

Pollard, Jack, *The Complete Illustrated History of Australian Cricket*, Viking, Melbourne 1995

Rosenwater, Irving, *Sir Donald Bradman: a Biography*, Batsford, London 1978

Whitington, R.S. and Hele, George, *Bodyline Umpire*, Rigby, Adelaide 1974

Williams, Charles, *Bradman – an Australian Hero*, Little, Brown and Company, London 1996

Newspapers and Periodicals
Barrier Miner (Broken Hill)
Canberra Times
Daily Mail (UK)
Dubbo Liberal
Evening News (Sydney)
Evening Standard (UK)
London Times
Newcastle Sun
Smith's Weekly
Southern Mail (Bowral)
Sydney Morning Herald
Sunday Dispatch (UK)
The Advertiser (Adelaide)

The Arrow (Sydney)
The Daily Telegraph (Sydney)
The Herald (Melbourne)
The News (Adelaide)
The Referee
The Sportsman
The Sun (Sydney)
The Truth (Sydney)
Western Champion (Parkes)

Online Resources

recordsearch.naa.gov.au
trove.nla.gov.au
rba.gov.au

www.ingramcontent.com/pod-product-compliance
Lightning Source LLC
Chambersburg PA
CBHW030231100526
44583CB00013BA/684